The Resume Writer's
WORKBOOK

Marketing Yourself throughout the Job Search Process

Third Edition

Stanley Krantman

DELMAR
CENGAGE Learning

Australia   Canada   Mexico   Singapore   Spain   United Kingdom   United States

The Resume Writer's Workbook:
Marketing Yourself throughout the
Job Search Process
Stanley Krantman

Vice President, Career Education SBU:
Dawn Gerrain

Director of Learning Solutions:
John Fedor

Managing Editor:
Robert L. Serenka, Jr.

Acquisitions Editor:
Martine Edwards

Editorial Assistant:
Falon Ferraro

Director of Production:
Wendy A. Troeger

Production Manager:
Mark Bernard

Content Project Manger:
Angela Iula

Production Assistant:
Matthew McGuire

Director of Marketing:
Wendy E. Mapstone

Channel Manager:
Gerard McAvey

Marketing Coordinator:
Jonathan Sheehan

Art Director:
Joy Kocsis

For product information and technology assistance, contact us at
Cengage Learning Customer & Sales Support, 1-800-354-9706

For permission to use material from this text or product,
submit all requests online at **cengage.com/permissions**
Further permissions questions can be emailed to
permissionrequest@cengage.com

Library of Congress Control Number: 2007022043

ISBN-13: 978-1-4180-6078-7

ISBN-10: 1-4180-6078-X

Delmar Cengage Learning
5 Maxwell Drive
Clifton Park, NY 12065-2919
USA

Cengage Learning products are represented in Canada by Nelson Education, Ltd.

For your lifelong learning solutions, visit **delmar.cengage.com**

Visit our corporate website at **www.cengage.com**

Notice to the Reader
Publisher does not warrant or guarantee any of the products described herein or perform any independent analysis in connection with any of the product information contained herein. Publisher does not assume, and expressly disclaims, any obligation to obtain and include information other than that provided to it by the manufacturer. The reader is expressly warned to consider and adopt all safety precautions that might be indicated by the activities described herein and to avoid all potential hazards. By following the instructions contained herein, the reader willingly assumes all risks in connection with such instructions. The publisher makes no representations or warranties of any kind, including but not limited to, the warranties of fitness for particular purpose or merchantability, nor are any such representations implied with respect to the material set forth herein, and the publisher takes no responsibility with respect to such material. The publisher shall not be liable for any special, consequential, or exemplary damages resulting, in whole or part, from the readers' use of, or reliance upon, this material.

Printed in the United States of America
6 7 8 12 11 10

The
Resume
Writer's
WORKBOOK

CONTENTS

Chapter 3: RESUME FORMAT • 13

Chapter 4: CONTACT INFORMATION • 19

Chapter 5: CAREER OBJECTIVE • 27

Chapter 6: SUMMARY OF QUALIFICATIONS • 37

Chapter 7: PROFESSIONAL EXPERIENCE—CHRONOLOGICAL • 43

Chapter 8: PROFESSIONAL EXPERIENCE—FUNCTIONAL • 59

Chapter 9: EDUCATION • 81

Chapter 10: ADDITIONAL QUALIFICATIONS • 91

Chapter 11: REFERENCES • 95

Chapter 12: PUTTING IT ALL TOGETHER • 101

Chapter 13: THE COVER LETTER • 109

Chapter 14: THE JOB APPLICATION AND SKILL TESTS • 119

Chapter 15: THE INTERNET AND YOUR JOB SEARCH • 129

Chapter 16: ELECTRONIC RESUMES, PORTFOLIOS, AND OTHER NEW RESUME FORMATS • 137

Chapter 17: NETWORKING • 151

Chapter 18: THE JOB INTERVIEW • 155

Chapter 19: YOUR PERSONAL JOB JOURNAL • 175

ACKNOWLEDGMENTS

I am sure most authors feel that once their book goes to print it is a finished product, thankfully never to be tampered with again. Unfortunately, the area of job search and resume writing is ever changing and what was true three years ago may not be true today. That's why a book of this nature is never "finished." In all fairness to the reader, a book on this topic demands to be revised every few years to reflect the changes and most recent trends. Keeping my book up to date has always been a top priority to me, and to Delmar Learning. I was enthusiastic when Delmar allowed me the opportunity to revise my book and I am proud to say that this third edition you now hold in your hands contains the most up-to-date information on each topic covered. Also in this new edition, I have incorporated information and topics that both readers and reviewers have requested, making this edition more "user friendly" and comprehensive.

I am deeply indebted to the many people who made this book possible. My former clients at Capital Writers, whose resumes I prepared, truly provided me with the experience and background that formed the foundation of this work. Also, the many people I interviewed for this edition, who gave freely of their time and advice, I thank you.

My deepest appreciation to the excellent staff at Delmar that painstakingly oversaw each phase of this revision, and whose attention to every detail resulted in a far better book than I would have produced on my own. In particular, I owe much thanks to Martine Edwards, Acquisitions Editor, whose enthusiasm for this project is the reason it was undertaken to begin with. Without her, this edition would never have been possible. She is a true professional.

Much thanks also to my excellent editor Falon Ferraro, whose sharp insights and suggestions not only made a significant contribution to this edition, but also made working on the revisions a truly enjoyable experience. I look forward to working with her again on other future projects.

To the excellent production staff, many whom I have not met personally but have seen their excellent work, I thank you. And last, but certainly not least, I would like to thank the many readers and reviewers—your advice has been invaluable and I thank all of you for your suggestions, many that I have incorporated into this edition.

Sara L. Morgan
Academic Advisor
Minnesota School of Business

Genine Longacker
School Counselor
Indian Lake Central School

Victoria Snabon-Heath
Associate Director of Career Services
International Academy of Design and Technology
Tampa, FL

David Parmenter
Corporate Director of Education
Wright Business School

Mary Gormandy White
Director and Co-Owner
Mobile Technical Institute

John Karras
Director, Career Services
Keller Graduate School of Management of DeVry University

Robert Giuffrida Jr., Ph.D.
Director for External Program Development
Mildred Elley School

Robin Delaney
Instructor, Hickey College

To all of you, my deepest appreciation. I couldn't have done it without you!

S.K.
St. Louis, 2007

INTRODUCTION

RECENT CHANGES IN THE JOB SEARCH MARKET

Since the publication of the second edition of this book, the job market has undergone many dynamic changes. While the resume and cover letter will always be a crucial and significant part of one's job search, today a good resume and cover letter are just not enough. Employers are becoming alarmed about the prevalence of resume padding, and consequently, they are now relying more on background checks, psychological testing, and intense interviews.

Many employers are becoming more suspicious of the accuracy of applicants' resumes. Moreover, the rising cost of hiring and training precludes employers from taking chances on candidates that are either inadequately qualified or lack a strong desire to remain with a company. Additionally, the number of resumes that employers receive is mounting, forcing employers to utilize various supplementary means for selection. While a good resume is still essential, it is no longer the single, foremost means employers use to screen applicants.

More emphasis is now placed on "Job Applications" and "Skill Tests." No longer regulated to entry-level positions, job applications are now required for many managerial and high-level positions. Today's job applications have become more complex and comprehensive, with questions ranging from job experience and skills to job performance—a topic traditionally addressed later in the interview.

Additionally, more employers are now adding psychometric or psychological tests to their pre-interview screening process. Aptitude testing, including problem-solving assessment, has become quite popular. To reflect these changes, this edition contains a new chapter on job applications and testing.

Interviewing has become more intricate and complex, as well. Here too, employers are taking a more aggressive approach. Interviews are no longer just "talking" about yourself and the job at hand, an increasing number of employers are utilizing "behavioral-based" interview questions. Many candidates are even undergoing a series of mock work assignments to simulate the daily pressure they will face in the job. This edition covers these new interview techniques, such as behavioral and case interviews, in more detail.

The role of the Internet in job search is also rapidly changing—for both the better and the worse. Fortuitously, more companies are managing their own dedicated Web sites where applicants can apply directly online for jobs. This has proven much more effective than the numerous generic job boards where hundreds of jobs and thousands of resumes reside. Getting to the source has always been one of the main principles of job search. Additionally, a company's own Web site can supply information about the working conditions and the job at hand to help the applicant decide whether the job interests him or her. This saves both the applicant and the company time.

Unfortunately, many generic job boards have been overwhelmed and others have proven to be a security threat. Today, applicants who post resumes on generic job boards may find themselves unknowingly victims of job scams and fraud, including identity theft. Important information regarding posting your resume safely on the Internet has been updated in this edition to reflect the changing role of the Web in today's job search.

A COMPLETE JOB SEARCH MANUAL

This workbook has evolved to reflect the continually changing job market. It is an *up-to-date*, *complete*, and *comprehensive* job search manual designed to guide you through every step. While many areas of job search may change, one thing always remains constant. Understanding how the job market works and mastering the various facets of job search (resumes, cover letters, networking, and interviewing) will give you the edge you need in this competitive market.

Remember, from the moment you send in your resume until the moment you are hired, you are being tested and compared. Every document, including your resume and application, will be scrutinized. Every interview question will be analyzed. You will be constantly compared to other applicants. Your skills and talent alone may be insufficient. You must always be prepared. This book will help you earn the dream job you deserve.

WHAT THIS WORKBOOK WILL DO FOR YOU

The Resume Writer's Workbook is designed to give you the edge you need in today's fiercely competitive job market. The structure of this workbook will simplify the arduous task of conducting a successful job search. Written clearly and concisely, the material is presented logically so that you can master it quickly. In practical terms, this workbook will help you

- ↷ produce a top-notch resume.
- ↷ write impressive cover letters.
- ↷ uncover solid job leads.
- ↷ use the Internet efficiently and *safely* in your job search.
- ↷ produce e-resumes and e-cover letters.
- ↷ create an impressive professional portfolio.
- ↷ effectively complete job applications.
- ↷ excel at interviews.
- ↷ follow up all interviews.
- ↷ keep detailed records of all leads.
- ↷ stay organized during your job search.

THE JOB SEARCH PROCESS

The material is presented in short, uncomplicated sections, and follows the logical sequence of the job search process.

Pre-Resume Preparation

- ↷ assessing skills
- ↷ deciding on a career objective

Resume Writing Process

- ↱ assembling all personal data
- ↱ selecting the most relevant information
- ↱ describing your skills, experience, and accomplishments effectively using powerful action verbs while emphasizing employer benefits
- ↱ printing the resume in an eye-catching layout
- ↱ preparing an e-resume (electronic or scannable version of your resume)

Post-Resume Preparation

- ↱ networking and selecting serious job leads
- ↱ submitting a resume and personalized cover letter to each prospective employer
- ↱ using the Internet to uncover leads and research employers' Web sites
- ↱ preparing a job application datasheet and effectively filling out applications
- ↱ interviewing for the job
- ↱ following up the interview
- ↱ keeping a detailed record of all contacts

THE WORKBOOK'S UNIQUE FORMAT

In the initial chapters you will assess your skills and career goals. You will be presented with the basics of conveying that information in an effective, high-power resume. Based on your skills, work experience, and career objectives, you will choose the best resume format for your individual needs.

Next, each component of the resume will be presented in a single, easy-to-read chapter. You will compose your resume one section at a time, directly in the workbook on the worksheet pages. Experience has proven that concentrating on each resume section individually simplifies the process and keeps the writing structured and focused.

Charts and worksheets have been provided to help you assemble and organize your information. Instruction sheets at the end of each chapter explain how to select your most impressive information.

After you have completed the worksheets, detach them. Chapter 12 describes how to organize and assemble the information. When you are ready to print your resume, the sample resumes at the end of the chapter will assist you in selecting an eye-catching layout.

Chapter 13 emphasizes the importance of a cover letter and demonstrates seven ways to make a cover letter effective. Sample cover letters, as well as important follow-up thank-you letters, are provided as models for constructing your own dynamic cover letters.

Chapter 14 discusses the increasingly important job application form. Applications are becoming more complex, and composing a comprehensive job application datasheet to help you effectively complete job application forms has become crucial. A worksheet will guide you through this process as well. A discussion about skill and aptitude tests, as well as psychometric personality testing, will help you understand what may confront you before or after an interview. While one cannot prepare for these tests, understanding the type of questions you will encounter will aid you in completing these tests to the best of your ability.

Chapter 15 gives updated information on the role of the Internet in job search and how it is changing. This chapter demonstrates how to use the Internet safely and effectively in a rapidly changing area of job search. It focuses on using the Web to network and to uncover job leads, as well as to take advantage of job boards and to research prospective employers' companies. Cautions and privacy concerns are also addressed. Additionally, you will discover how to use the Web in other areas of your job search to yield outstanding results.

Chapter 16 covers electronic resumes, or e-resumes. It explains how to prepare, format, and post them. Other contemporary job search tools such as professional portfolios and dedicated personal resume Web pages are also reviewed.

Chapter 17 elucidates proven techniques of networking to uncover hidden job markets. You will learn how to generate serious job leads and take advantage of them.

Chapter 18, on interviewing, will be an indispensable aid once your interviews become a reality. New interviewing techniques such as behavioral, stress, and case interviews are discussed. A mock interview, complete with the most frequently asked interview questions (and answers!) will provide you with the practice you will need to excel and outperform the competition.

Finally, Chapter 19 explains how a personal job journal will provide an excellent way to stay organized and keep track of all your leads.

Follow this workbook diligently and master these vital job search skills. They are your keys to obtaining the job you deserve. Best of luck in your endeavors!

Stan Krantman

The
Resume
Writer's
WORKBOOK

SKILL ASSESSMENT

YOUR ASSETS = YOUR SKILLS

Your value to an employer is directly proportional to the skills you have to offer. In the eyes of the employer, you are your skills.

Everyone has a unique combination of skills, and it's *your* unique combination that you are advertising in your resume. Therefore, before beginning your resume, taking inventory of your skills and clearly knowing what you have to offer is crucial.

Skills are not always technical, nor only acquired through formal education. Inborn personality traits and self-management skills are also meaningful to an employer; yet, most people tend to overlook these marketable traits when they prepare their resume.

Skills can also be acquired through experience—and not only employment experience. Often, volunteer duties can supply numerous skills for your inventory.

TRANSFERABLE SKILLS

Recently, "transferable skills" have received much attention. A transferable skill is simply a general skill used in one job situation that can be transferred to another job task without additional training.

For example, teachers utilize the skill of public speaking when addressing a class. This same public speaking skill can easily be transferred outside a classroom setting. Teachers could transfer this skill to a business setting and apply for a job training employees or conducting seminars.

If someone is proficient in a skill he or she enjoys, yet wants a change of jobs, then transferable skills should be stressed in the resume. Finding a job that fits his or her particular combination of skills would offer an excellent alternative.

DECIDING ON A CAREER GOAL

The first question you must ask yourself is: What job do I want? Without a specific goal or job objective, writing an effective resume and conducting an effective job search is impossible.

Choose a realistic job objective—a job for which you are currently qualified. In other words, you should be seeking a job that matches the skills you presently possess. In choosing a realistic objective the following three choices are open to you:

The Same Job You Just Left

Most unemployed people prefer to seek the same job they held previously. They are familiar with the work and already have the skills and experience for the necessary tasks.

A New Job—But One That Utilizes the Same General Skills

Many unemployed individuals opt for a change. The most logical job change would be one that utilizes the same skills in a different setting, such as the teachers mentioned in the previous section on transferable skills.

In this situation you would have to prepare a resume that highlights your transferable skills and demonstrates to a future employer that you are capable of transferring your skills to new tasks and responsibilities.

A Career Change

If you want to change careers, but do not have the skills or experience needed for the change, you can still implement a plan of action, such as one of the two below.

↪ You can return to school or begin an apprenticeship so that you can acquire the skills you need for your new career. This may require you to accept part-time work to make ends meet. However, if your goal is a new career, sacrificing the present to build a more satisfying future may be worthwhile.

↪ You can opt for an entry-level position in the area you desire. For example, you may decide that you are suited to be a manager but that you have no experience. If you cannot return to school to learn management skills, you could apply for an entry-level position in sales and learn the ropes while you acquire the necessary skills to advance to management.

If you decide to take an entry-level position, be sure your resume demonstrates that you are equipped with at least the minimal skills required to *begin* a career in your desired field. Taking an entry-level position and learning on the job offers an opportunity for you to make a career change a reality.

If you are uncertain of what skills are required for a career change, *do research*. Call people in the position you are seeking or call the personnel department and find out what skills are required for the job. If you can demonstrate in your resume that you have those skills, then you have an excellent chance at landing the job.

If you do not have the skills required, you will not get the job, and you will have to implement a career plan using your present skills.

The choice is yours. However, regardless of which course you decide to follow, it is imperative to identify your skills.

TAKING INVENTORY OF YOUR SKILLS

The practice worksheet at the end of this chapter will help you take inventory of your skills. Taking inventory before writing your resume is crucial. Doing so will keep you organized and focused as you write, and it will also aid you in setting a realistic career goal.

To inventory your skills, use the lists that precede the practice worksheet. The following instructions will explain how to use these lists in completing the practice worksheet that follows.

You may want to create your own skill areas such as Transportation Skills, and list such tasks as truck driving, chauffeur, and so forth.

The idea is to list *all* of your marketable skills—general and specific.

If you cannot find three major skill areas in which you are proficient, look at the tasks listed under each skill area. If you have performed any such tasks, list them.

CAUTION: **Many employers today are administering tests to verify applicants' skills. Be careful when listing skills (particularly technical skills) that you are not proficient at and will not perform well if tested.**

Technical Skills

Most of these are job titles. Check any of the positions on this list that you have held. Be sure to include volunteer work as well. If you were involved in fundraising for an organization, you may want to include skills such as bookkeeping, public relations, or sales and persuasion. Be thorough and list *everything*.

Next, prioritize these skills. List your strongest skills—those most important for your job objective—first. On the practice worksheet, under the heading Technical Skills, rank your top four skills from this list.

Major Skill Areas

These are general skills used in numerous jobs. These skills are also transferable. Check the ones you are proficient at. Next, prioritize them, and choose three main skill areas that are the most important for the job you are presently seeking. Write them on the practice worksheet in the spaces entitled Major Skill Areas.

SPECIFIC TASKS

Under each major skill area, you will find a list of specific tasks. Check the tasks you have performed. Prioritize them. Then add them to your practice worksheet. Be sure the tasks you record correspond to one of the major skill areas you have listed.

Marketable Personality Traits

What are your most marketable personality traits and self-management skills? Most marketable means those that are most in demand for your job goal and are most impressive to your future employer.

If the job you are seeking is people oriented, be sure to emphasize people-oriented traits. Naturally, such traits as "loyal," "dependable," and "works well under pressure," are qualities employers always seek.

Again, be selective and prioritize. If you are seeking a job as a manager, you may want to emphasize skills such as ability to motivate people, getting along with others, and being a team player. Conversely, accountants would emphasize task-oriented goals, because their job primarily deals with data, not people. They may want to stress such traits as being analytical, having an eye for detail, and working well under pressure.

CAUTION: **Personality traits are subjective—not clearly black or white. Be sure you can support each trait with experience (professional or nonprofessional) or with recommendations from others.**

Once again, select your three most marketable traits, and list them on your practice worksheet.

Technical Skill Areas

Account Management
Accounting
Administration
Administrative Assistant
Adult Care
Advertising
Appraising
Arc Welding
Architect
Artist–Illustrator
Assembly Line Work
Audio-Visual
Auditing
Automotive
Banking
Barber
Bookkeeping
Broker
Building Maintenance
Business Management
Buyer
Capital Development
Career Development
Carpenter
Cash-Flow Management
Cashier–Checkout
Chemistry
Child Care
Clergy
Clerk
Communications
Community Relations
Computer Sciences
Conservationist
Construction–Labor
Consulting
Consumer Affairs
Corporate Executive
Cost Analysis
Counseling
Curriculum Development
Customer Relations
Data Processing
Delivery
Department Manager
Designing
Development
Dietician
Drafting
Drama
Driving
Editor/Editing
Education
Electronics

Employee Relations
Engineering
Equipment Maintenance
Farm Work
Fashion/Clothing
Field Research
Filing
Film/Video
Finance
Fitness Consultant
Flight Attendant
Food Preparation
Food Services
Foreign Languages
Forklifting
Franchise Management
Gardening
Geology
Government Service
Graphic Design
Groundskeeping
Health Sciences
Hotel Management
Housekeeping
Import/Export
Insurance
Interior Design
International Business
Interviewing
Inventory Control
Jeweler
Journalism
Laboratory Technician
Legal Services
Loading/Unloading
Loans
Machine Operation
Mail Clerk
Make-up/Cosmetology
Management
Market Research
Marketing
Mathematician
Medical Services
Military
Modeling
Municipal Work
Music
Nurse
Office Management
Performing Arts
Pharmaceutical
Photographer
Physical Therapist

Physicist
Plumber
Police/Security
Printing
Product Development
Product Management
Proofreading
Psychologist
Public Relations
Publishing
Purchasing
Quality Control
Radio
Real Estate
Receptionist
Recruiting
Recycling
Remodeling
Repairing
Reporting
Research and Development
Retail Sales
Robotics
Sales Representative
Secretarial
Securities
Security Guard
Social Worker
Special Education
Speech Pathologist
Sports
Statistics
Supervisor
Switchboard
Systems Analysis
Teacher
Telecommunications
Therapy
Trade Shows
Training
Transportation
Travel Agent
Truck Driver
Veterinarian
Visual Arts
Volunteer Services
Waiter/Waitress
Warehouse Work
Waste Disposal
Word Processing
Writer
Other: _____
_____
_____

Major Skill Areas   Specific Tasks

Management Skills

Administering
Analyzing performance
Coordinating programs
Delegating responsibility
Evaluating performance
Executing programs
Improving techniques
Increasing sales
Monitoring people and tasks
Motivating people
Organizing people and tasks
Planning
Prioritizing
Recruiting and hiring
Reorganizing
Restructuring
Reviewing
Scheduling
Supervising

Communication Skills

Addressing the public
Advising people
Arbitrating
Arranging functions
Coaching
Correspondence
Counseling
Directing people and tasks
Editing
Entertaining people
Fundraising
Handling complaints
Instructing
Lecturing
Meeting the public
Moderating
Negotiating
Persuading
Promoting events
Publicizing products
Public relations
Recruiting
Running meetings
Selling
Setting up demonstrations

Teaching
Translating
Writing press releases

Research Skills

Analyzing
Calculating
Clarifying
Compiling statistics
Evaluating programs
Indexing
Organizing programs and data
Summarizing
Systematizing

Financial Skills

Appraising
Auditing financial records
Balancing
Billing (A/P, A/R)
Bookkeeping
Budget management
Calculating
Computing
Forecasting trends
Invoicing
Payroll
Preparing taxes
Projecting future growth
Purchasing
Raising funds

Creative Skills

Conceptualizing
Creating new ideas and products
Designing
Developing new techniques
Establishing
Founding
Illustrating
Implementing
Integrating
Introducing
Inventing
Originating
Performing

Planning
Revitalizing

Clerical Skills

Arranging functions
Basic computer skills
Billing
Calculating
Cataloguing and filing
Compiling information
Coordinating itineraries
Correspondence
Dispatching
Editing reports/letters
Generating information
Monitoring
Organizing office
Prioritizing
Reading materials
Scheduling appointments
Systematizing information
Taking dictation
Typing
Writing reports

Computer Skills

Creating new software
Designing new systems
Entering data
Knowledge of programs:
    Accounting programs
    Database programs
    Languages (C, Java, etc.)
    Spreadsheet programs
    Word processing programs
Maintaining computers
Operating systems
Programming
Repairing systems

Other Skills

_____
_____
_____
_____
_____
_____

Marketable Personality Traits

Task-Oriented Skills

Accurate
Adaptable
Ambitious
Analytical
Artistic
Aware (i.e., of market trends)
Capable
Clear-thinking
Committed to growth
Competent
Conscientious
Creative
Dedicated
Dependable
Eager
Efficient
Energetic
Enterprising
Eye for detail
Farsighted
Flexible
Goal directed
Good judgment
Hardworking
High achiever
High energy
Highly motivated
Honest
Imaginative
Independent
Industrious
Innovative
Leadership ability
Loves a challenge
Loyal
Manages time efficiently
Methodical
Meticulous
Motivated
Optimistic
Orderly
Organized
Perfectionist
Persistent

Problem solver
Productive
Punctual
Quick learner
Realistic
Reliable
Resourceful
Risk taker
Self-motivated
Sensitive
Serious
Shrewd
Sincere
Team player
Thorough
Trustworthy
Verbal
Versatility
Visionary
Works well under pressure

People-Oriented Skills

Ability to motivate others
Communicative
Congenial
Cooperative
Courteous
Diplomatic
Eloquent
Friendly
Generous
Gets along well with others
Good listener
Helpful
Leadership qualities
Outgoing
Patience
Sense of humor
Sensible
Supportive
Sympathetic
Team worker
Tolerant
Understanding

CHAPTER 1   WORKSHEET

Skill Inventory Practice

Technical Skills:

1. _____
2. _____
3. _____
4. _____

Major Skill Areas:

1. _____

2. _____

3. _____

Specific Skills:

A. _____
B. _____
C. _____
A. _____
B. _____
C. _____
A. _____
B. _____
C. _____

Personality Traits:

1. _____
2. _____
3. _____

THE IMPORTANCE OF A RESUME

WHY YOU NEED A RESUME

In today's job market, the resume has become the number one item potential employers request. Before an employer will take valuable time to interview you, he or she wants to meet you—on paper. Impressing that employer with your resume can, and will, make all the difference.

The term *résumé* comes from the French and means a "summary." Your resume is exactly that: a summary of your qualifications, skills, and achievements. It shows a future employer what you have done. It details your skills, training, work experience, education, and most importantly, your accomplishments with past employers.

It should also inform the employer of your career objective (the job you are seeking) and communicate in a concise manner the benefits of hiring you.

Without a resume you cannot compete, and an inferior resume will eliminate you before you even have a chance. Therefore, having a superior resume—one that effectively displays to employers what you can do for them—is imperative.

YOUR RESUME IS A "MARKETING TOOL"

You should think of your resume as an advertisement—one that advertises *you* to a future employer. What you are "selling" is your unique combination of skills, qualifications, experience, and personality. All of these qualities must be obvious in your resume. You can impress an employer by creating a resume that exhibits the *benefits* you have to offer, rather than merely enumerating a shopping list of skills. A resume that focuses on employer benefits, not just skills, will rise above the competition.

EMPLOYER BENEFITS VERSUS SUMMARY OF SKILLS

A resume should be results driven rather than skills driven. By reading your resume, the employer must *quickly* understand what advantages you offer his or her company. Think of yourself as a product and the employer as the consumer. How would you sell your product (yourself) to the employer?

When a leading soap manufacturer came up with a new formula for its detergent, it told the public it had added a new ingredient, green crystals, and mentioned the scientific name. Ingredients and technical jargon mean little to the consumer. What sold the product was the manufacturer's claim that these crystals made clothes cleaner and brighter. Whether you are selling soap or your services, people want to know the bottom line: What can you do to improve their situation, what can you offer; in other words, why should they hire *you*.

An employer is more interested in the benefits you offer than in your impressive repertoire of skills. When you write your resume, highlight these employer benefits. For example, if you are proficient in desktop publishing, do not just list your skills or the computer programs you've mastered. Translate those skills into benefits. Tell the employer what you are able to do with your desktop publishing skills. Instead of stating, "proficient in Microsoft Publisher," state "ability to produce attractive brochures at a low cost."

Skills only indicate your *potential*, while benefits demonstrate your *actual accomplishments*—what you have achieved with your skills. An employer realizes that many applicants are well-versed in desktop publishing. Impressing the employer with what you have done and can do with your skills will propel you past the competition.

For another example, pretend you are proficient in spreadsheets. However, if you created a nifty phone/address book from a simple spreadsheet, this will certainly impress an employer. Many people can enter data on a spreadsheet, but demonstrating how you used this skill to accomplish a task efficiently will distinguish your resume.

Determine which benefits are most important to your target employer, and then stress them in your resume. Remember, while many people have the same skills you do, few will translate those skills into benefits on their resume. Stay ahead of the competition by ensuring that your resume highlights those important employer benefits you have to offer.

Benefits and accomplishments also help an employer visualize how you will perform on the job. The better an employer feels he or she can predict your performance, the greater your chances are of getting an interview.

Translate Your Skills into Employer Benefits

Look at the worksheet from Chapter 1. Try to take each of the skills you mentioned and translate them into a benefit or accomplishment. The more specific it is, the better it is. These are the benefits and accomplishments you will want to focus on and include in your resume. Even your personality traits can be translated into accomplishments. Your "eye for detail" may be responsible for emending spelling errors in important documents. Investigate each skill similarly to produce concrete benefits you can offer the employer.

Skill: Accomplishment/Benefit:

1. _____

2. _____

3. _____

4. _____

Personality Trait: Accomplishment/Benefit:

1. _____

2. _____

3. _____

4. _____

HIGH-TECH BRINGS NEW CHANGES TO RESUMES

Today's workplace is becoming increasingly competitive. Changing jobs has become a way of life. Many companies are downsizing to save money, and thus more people, even those with solid backgrounds and skills, are looking for work. Additionally, many people become quickly dissatisfied with their jobs and look for new ones. Moreover, the increasing number of Internet job boards has enabled thousands of applicants to answer each job ad. Now more than ever, you need a top-notch resume to put you above the competition. Your resume must stand out or you will be lost in the shuffle.

THE PURPOSE OF THE RESUME IS TO GET YOU AN INTERVIEW

Most people think that a good resume will get them a job. This is a mistake. Finding an employer today who hires anyone solely on what he or she has read in a resume is unheard of. Employers want to meet you in person before they hire you. They want you to substantiate the facts in your resume, and they want to be convinced you have the right personality. This requires an interview. It's the interview that ultimately gets you the job.

However, it's the resume that gets you the interview! In today's market, where many companies utilize resume-tracking programs that rely on a computer to select your resume based on keywords, you must be extra careful to fill your resume with benefits. You not only have to impress the employer, you must impress his or her computer as well! The purpose of any resume, electronic or otherwise, is simply to get you an interview.

How often have you thought, "If only I had met with the employer in person, I could have convinced him that I was the right person for the job!" Your only chance is to compose an impressive resume, one that the employer will notice, so that you can meet the employer in person and get the job.

OTHER REASONS FOR A RESUME

Although the main purpose of the resume is to get you an interview, other important reasons exist to create a resume.

- ↝ **Prepare yourself for the interview.** Most employers will use your resume as a guideline when they interview you. They will ask you to explain in detail the statements you have made in your resume.

- ↝ **Organize yourself.** Preparing a resume forces you to assess your skills. This in turn will help you evaluate the many employment options open to you. It will also help you plan an effective job search campaign.

- ↝ **Let employers know that you are actively seeking employment.**

- ↝ **Give yourself a sense of security.** Always having an updated resume is a good idea. You never know when you will want to seek a better job or just a change. Furthermore, in case you unexpectedly lose your job, having your resume updated and ready is wise.

- ↝ **Have a calling card.** It is there when you want to conduct informational interviews to test potential opportunities. (See Chapter 17, Networking.)

WRITING AN EFFECTIVE RESUME

Most positions generate hundreds of resume responses. Employers cannot read them all! Consequently, they will scan the resumes. You sometimes have less than 15 seconds to make that all-important first impression. Therefore, your resume must be distinct! Even in today's high-tech market where computers evaluate the resumes, after a resume is chosen, the hiring manager will eventually read it. Thus, it must be impressive.

To ensure that your resume stands out in the crowd, concentrate on the three most essential factors in writing your resume:

Select Your Most Powerful and Impressive Information

Selectivity is the key to writing a strong resume. You have only one chance to make a first impression, so you must give it your best shot. Do not bore the reader with endless facts about your past employment. Your resume is neither an obituary nor a biography—it is an ad. Like you would with an ad, write to impress. Present only *significant* information about your professional experience.

Your most significant and impressive information will answer the employer's primary question: Why should I hire you?

Your resume must communicate that you will be an asset to the organization. It should reveal you as a problem solver with important benefits to offer.

Be concise. Focus only on your achievements and skills that are required for the job you are seeking. Eliminate extra information that detracts from emphasizing what the job requires. With a resume, less is more.

How does one know which skills and benefits to highlight and select? Do research. Find out what problems come with the job. Find out the qualifications the employer is seeking. Talking to personnel and reading the want ads carefully will give you a sufficient idea. Demonstrate to the employer that you are the person he or she is seeking.

Write with Impact

Use action verbs to describe your accomplishments. Action verbs conjure up a positive image in the employer's mind and give you an advantage. Action verbs describe you as a person who accomplishes goals.

Action verbs are also more concise and make your resume more readable. A detailed discussion of action verbs and how to use them appears in Chapters 7 and 8.

For electronic resumes, keywords count. These are usually nouns, buzzwords, or catchphrases used to describe your job and level of proficiency. Chapter 16 will show you how to select powerful keywords.

Use an Eye-Catching Layout

The best resumes are one page long. If you have much experience, you may require two pages. However, under no circumstances should a resume be longer than two pages. The more concise it is the better. Your most pertinent information should stand out with either all caps (capital letters), boldface, or italics. You may also use bullets (•) to draw the reader's attention to significant information.

Electronic resumes have their own unique layout to accommodate for ASCII text, which is more easily read and scanned by a computer. Today having both versions of your resume accessible is imperative.

The following chapters will help guide you through the resume-writing process with easy-to-follow, step-by-step instructions and worksheets. Complete each chapter and you will have a professional quality resume, one that will impress an employer and be your ticket to an interview.

CHAPTER 3

RESUME FORMAT

CHRONOLOGICAL VERSUS FUNCTIONAL FORMAT

To explain the two most widely acceptable resume formats used today, we employ the example of Juan Ortega.

In 1999, Juan began working for Capital Corporation as a sales representative. His job was to sell software packages to high-profile clients such as AT&T. In 2002, he began his own business as a computer consultant. His business failed and he is now looking for a job as a computer consultant for a large firm.

Below are two ways that Juan can present his employment history.

EXAMPLE: **CHRONOLOGICAL FORMAT**

2002 to Present
   CEO/President, Ortega & Associates
   • Designed and maintained hardware systems
   • Evaluated and implemented software

1999 to 2002
   Sales Representative, Capital Corp.
   • Designed program sales packages for large companies such as AT&T
   • Increased gross sales by 10 percent

EXAMPLE: **FUNCTIONAL FORMAT**

COMPUTER CONSULTING AND DESIGN
   • Designed and implemented hardware and software systems for large industries
   • Evaluated computer software

SALES AND SERVICE
   • Experienced sales representative, whose clients included AT&T and McDonalds
   • Developed marketing plan for Ortega & Associates, resulting in a 10% sales increase in 2006
   • Evaluated software packages for large corporations

2002 to Present   CEO, Ortega & Associates
1999 to 2002   Sales Representative, Capital Corp.

Look at the examples of Juan Ortega's work history. What are the main differences between the chronological format and the functional format? Both formats give Juan's background and experience. Both mention his skills and accomplishments.

The difference between them is emphasis; namely, what is accentuated and what is mentioned first.

The chronological format stresses

↱ dates and lengths of jobs.

↱ past employers.

↱ job titles.

The functional resume stresses

↱ skill areas.

↱ qualifications.

Glancing at the chronological resume, we see immediately that Juan was CEO of a corporation. This can be very impressive. Additionally, if Capital Corp. is a large, well-known firm, seeing Juan's relationship to that company would also be impressive. Initially, you may think that this makes the chronological format a good choice.

However, Juan has had two different jobs in a short time span. Looking at his experience from a time frame does not show a strong, steady work background. If he had worked for Capital Corp. seven or eight years, then the chronological format, which would stress his ability to stick with a job, would have been preferable. In reality, he held his present job for less than two years.

Therefore, his best choice is to emphasize his accomplishments, which are impressive. In this situation, the functional resume, which stresses his skills and accomplishments, would be the better way to present his experience and background.

One advantage of the functional resume is that Juan can choose which of his skills to place first. If he were seeking another job in sales, he would place his sales skills first, even though his last job was not in sales. In the chronological resume, Juan would have to place his last job first regardless of his present career objective.

It is important to note, however, that even in the functional format Juan listed his dates of employment and the names of his past employers. Many who follow a strictly functional format will omit this information. Be warned: Your future employer will want to know whom you have worked for and how long you have worked for them. If you do not have it on your resume, you can expect that question at the interview. Worse, most employers expect to see this information on your resume. If it is missing they get suspicious, and they may even think you are hiding something. If an employer entertains such a suspicion, he or she may choose not to even bother with you and may refuse an interview. Employers want evidence that you have the skills you claim. They want to know where you got those skills and for whom you made your accomplishments. Therefore, be safe and include this information on your resume.

With the functional format you still have an advantage. By mentioning your skills first and putting the emphasis on your skill areas, your employer will be favorably impressed before finishing your resume. When he or she finally reads your chronology, not holding one job for a long period is less likely to be an issue.

SELECTING THE RIGHT FORMAT FOR YOUR RESUME

To help you choose the format that best suits your needs, look at the two charts that follow. One lists the advantages of using the chronological format, while the other lists the advantages of the functional format.

Read the charts. Check the statements that apply to you. If you can see a pattern (most of your check marks fall in the same chart), then your choice of format is clear.

Some people have multiple job objectives and find that numerous statements in both charts are true for them. If you are pursuing a job in two diverse areas, you will need two different resumes.

For example, you may be thinking about a career change, and decide to apply for a job in a new but related field. Although you do not have any solid work experience in this new area, you do have the skills required for the job. Therefore, a functional resume that stresses your transferable skills would be the most appropriate. However, like most people, you worry you may not get an interview due to your lack of experience. Therefore, to be safe, you also seek a job in your present career. For that, a chronological resume that stresses your present job title and your most recent accomplishments would serve you best. In this situation, two resumes are better than one.

Chronological Format

- ☐ I have held the same job for more than five years.
- ☐ My employment history is one of stability. I rarely change jobs.
- ☐ My past employer(s) is a prestigious company, well-known in my field.
- ☐ My job titles are impressive.
- ☐ I plan to continue in the same field as my past job.
- ☐ I have considerable experience but in one area only.
- ☐ I have a limited repertoire of skill areas.

Functional Format

- ☐ I am changing careers.
- ☐ I have never held one job for a long time.
- ☐ I recently finished school and do not have any professional experience.
- ☐ I am reentering the job force after a considerable absence.
- ☐ I am proficient in many areas and have many skills.
- ☐ I have held many jobs in various unrelated work areas.
- ☐ Most of my work experience has been freelance or temporary.
- ☐ My skills fit in better with my present career objective than do my prior job titles.

SECTION HEADINGS

Before you begin writing your resume, having an overview of the standard, acceptable resume format is important.

The format is simple. Think of your resume as an outline of your professional capabilities. As such, the resume is divided into outline headings or sections. These standard, general sections are on all resumes and are guidelines in organizing your particular information.

These headings allow the employer to quickly scan a resume for pertinent information. Furthermore, because these headings have become standard protocol, employers expect to find them on your resume. Thus, you should not deviate from this format.

The following chart lists and defines these standard headings. Some of them, such as Summary of Qualifications, are optional. However, many optional sections are becoming common in resumes, and including them in your resume is usually best.

Resume Headings

Contact Information

Name, address, phone numbers, and e-mail address.
This informs employers how to reach you for an interview.

Career Objective

It is the exact job title of the position sought.

Summary of Qualifications

It contains short highlights of your most impressive qualifications for the job.
This can be anything from skill areas and accomplishments to personality traits.

Professional Experience—*Chronological Resume*

This is a list of all past employment, starting with your most recent employer.
Gives job titles and lists under each a short description of your tasks and accomplishments for that job.

Skill Areas—*Functional Resume*

Your general skill areas are section headings.
Under each skill area list specific job tasks and accomplishments that demonstrate your proficiency in that skill area.

Education

Highlight your most recent degree, and the colleges or trade schools you attended.
List any awards, dean's lists, or school projects that pertain to your career objective.
If you do not have a college education, mention your high school and diploma.

Additional Personal Information

Mention only that personal information that pertains to your job objective.
For example: awards, professional associations, and publications.

HOW TO ORGANIZE THE HEADINGS

How do you organize the headings? As mentioned earlier, emphasis is the key. What would impress your future employer more, your work experience or your education?

If you are a recent graduate with limited professional experience, then your education would be more impressive, and you would want to emphasize it. Therefore, the Education heading would go before the Experience heading.

What if you have a strong work history but your most outstanding achievements are from jobs *previous* to your last one? What do you stress, your steady work history (chronological format) or your achievements (functional format)? You are worried that if you follow the chronological format, and list your last job first, your more impressive qualifications will be buried. In this case, you can use the more acceptable chronological format but include a short Summary of Qualifications to emphasize your most impressive accomplishments and skills first.

In short, section headings that contain your most important and impressive information should be listed first.

WHAT MUST *NEVER* GO IN A RESUME

Unfortunately, many employers examine resumes in hopes of finding flaws. Due to the large number of applications, employers may use the resume as a tool to eliminate prospective applicants—rather than one for choosing the right person for the job. Everyone understands that a resume that fails to depict the applicant as having the skills for the job will eliminate him or her from the competition.

However, people fail to realize that mentioning negative information (facts that bother the employer) can eliminate even the most highly qualified applicant.

How do you protect yourself? Never offer too much information. Keep your resume focused on your skills and accomplishments. Never mention personal information, controversial information, or anything negative about yourself. Never mention your race or religion. Marital status and political affiliations are also not pertinent to your job performance. Never mention salary requirements or reasons for leaving a prior job. Although these issues may come up in the interview, the resume is not the place for this information.

Never Mention

- race
- political affiliations
- religion
- salary requirements
- marital status
- reasons for leaving a past job

GETTING STARTED

The division of a resume into section headings makes it easier to write. The headings give you a system for organizing your information and allow you to focus on the most pertinent facts.

Once you have selected your format, chronological or functional, and the order of your section headings, you merely organize your particular information accordingly.

This workbook is designed to simplify your task. It is divided into the same sections as your resume.

It will guide you through each section of your resume, one at a time, and show you how to select the most important information in your unique background that applies to that section. It will also aid you in presenting your information with impact and using the right action verbs to express your talents best.

Remember, your resume must make an impact to attract attention. Follow this workbook, step by step, and you will have a resume that gets noticed.

Let us begin writing.

CHAPTER 4

CONTACT INFORMATION

Name, Address, Phone Number(s), E-Mail Address, Web-Page Hyperlink

This is the information an employer needs in order to contact you for an interview.

Your contact information is the most important information on your resume. If the employer has no idea how to reach you, you will not get an interview, regardless of your excellent resume and qualifications. Check and double check that your address and phone number are correct!

The first thing an employer looks at is your contact headline. Thus, projecting a professional image from the start is crucial! Use an attractive layout. (See the examples that follow.)

Design a letterhead you can use in all your business correspondence, such as cover letters and follow-up letters.

HOW TO PRESENT YOUR CONTACT INFORMATION

Name

1. Use your full name—first and last. Do not add nicknames or titles, such as John Doe III, unless you use them professionally. The idea is to project a professional image, not a lax, overly friendly or a high-strung, overly formal one.

2. Make your name stand out. Use capital letters and/or boldface type. If you have a word processor, you may want to use a larger point size for your name.

3. Disambiguate your name. If your name can be either masculine or feminine, such as Francis, you may want to add Mr. or Ms. in front of your name (Ms. Francis Smith), to spare your employer from a possibly awkward situation.

Address

1. Use a permanent address. Do not use post office boxes or addresses that imply you are a transient. Again, project a professional image.

2. Do not use abbreviations, because they can be confusing. Spell out everything (including Street, not St., and the like). The exception to this rule is the two-letter abbreviation for your state, which is the post office standard.

3. Put city, state, and zip code on one line. Be sure to put a comma between the city and state. Make sure your zip code is correct.

Phone Number

1. Use your area code—your resume could be sent out of town for review.

2. Leave a daytime phone number. This is important because most employers will want to contact you during business hours. Be sure someone is present to receive calls. If no one can be there, or if you do not want calls at your workplace, hire an answering service or set up an answering machine. If an employer calls and no one is there to receive the call, you may not get another chance. Additionally, list your evening (home) number.

3. Consider including your fax number, if you have one. Be sure to indicate which number is your home phone and which number is your fax line. Thus, you could have three telephone numbers listed on your resume: daytime phone, evening phone (home phone), and fax line.

4. Consider your cell phone. If you have a mobile or cell phone and you want to receive calls on that line, be sure to add it as well. However, listing too many numbers on your resume is dangerous. If possible, limit the number to three: daytime, evening, and fax. Use your cell for either daytime or evening and a second number of your choice.

Phone Etiquette

Always project a professional image. This means that when an employer calls your home phone, he or she should not be greeted with a cutesy phone message or one where your precocious three-year-old announces that you are not at home. Be professional at all times. If needed, get a dedicated phone line reserved for your job search. Projecting a professional image cannot be overstressed, as it can make the difference in getting an interview.

E-Mail Address

1. Give an e-mail address. In today's high-tech society, it is important to have an e-mail address and to include it in your contact information. Many employers prefer to contact applicants via e-mail.

2. List your e-mail address instead of your fax number if your contact information is lengthy. Usually e-mail is preferred over fax (it is quicker, more reliable, and the copies are cleaner and easier to read).

3. Write your e-mail address in all lowercase and in a smaller point size than the rest of your contact information. See Example 1 for how it should look.

4. Double check your spelling, as it is very easy to transpose letters. Remember, one typo or even a wrong period (.) could result in losing the job because the employer could not contact you.

5. Get a free Web-based e-mail, if necessary. If you do not own a computer, or if you are planning on changing commercial Internet service providers, subscribe to a service such as Windows Live Hotmail <http://www.hotmail.com> or Yahoo! Mail <http://mail.yahoo.com>. These free services allow you to access your e-mail from any computer with an Internet connection, and do not require a special Internet service provider's account.

E-MAIL ETIQUETTE

As with your answering machine messages, projecting a professional image is imperative. Therefore, your e-mail address must project a professional image as well. E-mail addresses such as "redhotmama14" or "hoosiersrus" do not impress an employer. Use a simple e-mail address, such as a combination of your first and last name or your last name followed by a number. The purpose is to be professional at all times!

Web-Page Hyperlink

1. Consider including your Web site, if you have a dedicated one. Many programs, such as Microsoft Word, will automatically add a hyperlink to a Web page. This means that if an employer downloads your e-resume, he or she only needs to click on your hyperlink to go to your Web page.

2. Make your Web site viewable for a wider audience. Many people prefer to furnish Web site information in a cover letter so that they can better control who accesses their Web site. (See Example 5.) However, you may opt to have your Web-page resume open to all and password protect only those pages (such as Letters of Recommendation) that you want to give limited access to. When you do want an employer to view those pages, you can simply send an e-mail to him or her with the password.

EXAMPLES

The following are examples of ways to handle your contact information.

Study the different layouts and choose one that appeals to you. Any one of them would be a good choice for your resume and letterhead.

EXAMPLE 1: MOST COMMON LAYOUT

This has become the most common layout, and you will not go wrong with it.

JUAN ORTEGA
1124 Bakery Avenue
Bakersville, NC 90000
(555) 876-7876
juano@sbcglobal.net

EXAMPLE 2: ANOTHER POPULAR LAYOUT

Arranging your name on the far right has a definite advantage. When an employer flips through a stack of resumes, yours will distinguish itself. Thus, some experts prefer this layout.

> **JUAN ORTEGA**
> 1124 Bakery Avenue
> Bakersville, NC 90000
> (555) 876-7876
> juano@sbcglobal.net

EXAMPLE 3: A VARIATION OF THE PREVIOUS LAYOUT

This layout is pleasing to the eye only if all of your resume headings are left justified.

> **JUAN ORTEGA**
> 1124 Bakery Avenue
> Bakersville, NC 90000
> (555) 876-7876
> juano@sbcglobal.net

EXAMPLE 4: ANOTHER VARIATION

This is a nice layout if you want to put emphasis on your phone number. It is especially effective if you are listing more than one number.

> **JUAN ORTEGA**
> 1124 Bakery Avenue
> Bakersville, NC 90000
>
> Day Phone: (555) 876-7876
> Home Phone: (555) 887-9087
> juano@sbcglobal.net

EXAMPLE 5: A CONTEMPORARY LAYOUT

> **JUAN ORTEGA**
> 1124 Bakery Avenue • Bakersville, NC 90000 • (555) 876-7876
> Web site: http://umo.edu/juan12.html

EXAMPLE 6: ANOTHER VARIATION

This format is an excellent choice. It highlights your name, and because it is so different, your resume immediately stands out from the others. It also makes for a professional-looking letterhead.

> 1124 Bakery Avenue
> Bakersville, NC 90000
> (555) 876-7876
> juano@sbcglobal.net
>
> **JUAN ORTEGA**

WORKSHEET INSTRUCTIONS

Enter your contact information as you want it to appear on your resume.

Study the examples on the preceding pages. Choose one. Arrange your information according to that layout.

Use a font that stands out, such as Times Roman, Bookman, Palatino, or any other serif font. (The serif fonts are easier to read than sans serif fonts, such as Helvetica.)

For effect, use bold or italic fonts, or even all caps. You may also change the point size of a font to highlight your name. For example, you may want your name in 16-point type and boldface, and the rest of the contact information in 12-point type. This way, your name stands out.

When you have finished, check and double check that your

- address and zip code are correct.
- area code is listed with the phone number.
- day phone and home phone are both listed if needed.
- e-mail address is typed correctly.

CHAPTER 4

WORKSHEET

Contact Information

Contact Information:

_____

_____

_____

_____

_____

_____

Resume Style Guidelines:

Name should be:	**Address should be:**	**Phone Number should be:**
☐ All caps	☐ All caps	☐ All caps
☐ Boldface	☐ Boldface	☐ Boldface
☐ Italics	☐ Italics	☐ Italics
☐ Centered	☐ Centered	☐ Centered
☐ Right aligned	☐ Right aligned	☐ Right aligned
☐ Left aligned	☐ Left aligned	☐ Left aligned
☐ Point size _____	☐ Point size _____	☐ Point size _____

Other Instructions:

☐ E-mail address

☐ Hyperlink to Web site

CAREER OBJECTIVE

> **Specific job title of the position you are seeking**
>
> - This information indicates the job for which you are applying.
> - It gives your resume a focal point, around which all the remaining information will be organized.
> - An *effective objective* not only lists the prospective job title, but also informs employers of what you plan to do for them and/or of the benefits you have to offer them.

CAREER OBJECTIVE: IS IT REQUIRED OR OPTIONAL?

Resume "experts" disagree about whether a Career Objective should be included in a resume.

Some experts feel that omitting the objective is best. They reason that if it is too specific, employers will not consider you for any other job outside your objective, even though other available jobs may be suitable. If it is too general, it appears that you do not know what you want to do. Therefore, they think it best to include your objective and career goals in your cover letter.

Most experts do not agree with this opinion. Most think the career objective is a *must*. By not including it, you give the impression of being undecided about your career goals. This is especially true if you do a functional resume. Without an objective, a functional resume will lack focus and be confusing because you are listing your skill areas instead of your job titles. The employer will not know what job you are seeking, and may discard your resume altogether. Conversely, stating an objective shows that you know what you want. It demonstrates to the employer that you are goal oriented and serious about your career. By including this information, you present a professional image. Once more, it cannot be stressed enough that in a resume, *image is everything!*

My personal experience has proven that stating your career objective is important. In today's market, many employers will have a member of personnel scan and file all incoming resumes. If there is no objective, personnel maybe unsure of how to file your resume, and it will go directly into the circular file—the garbage can.

Furthermore, many companies have multiple positions open simultaneously. Without an objective, the employer may be unsure which position you are applying for and consequently not bother with your resume.

It sounds cruel, but put yourself in the employer's position. Most job openings generate hundreds of resumes. Who has time to read them all? Thus, most employers initially scan them for keywords and pertinent information rather than carefully reading them. If they are intrigued, your resume will go into a pile for further consideration. If they do not find a catch word or a specific job title they are looking for, the employers will not consider your resume at all.

As you will discover in Chapter 16, many companies now use computers to evaluate and select resumes. These resume-tracking systems search a resume for keywords, in particular job titles and objectives. Electronic resumes posted on Internet job boards and e-resumes sent via e-mail are almost always assessed by a computer. Most of them are catalogued by the "objective." Thus, including an objective is imperative.

When you find a specific job opening that interests you, you can customize your resume for it by changing just one line—your career objective. With today's simple word processing programs, multiple resumes, each with different objectives, can be produced with just a few easy keystrokes.

While adding an objective may limit your chances of getting any job, it will infinitely increase your chances of getting the job you want! In short, include your objective, but make it professional and effective!

HOW TO WRITE YOUR CAREER OBJECTIVE

Simple Objective

You can handle the objective on your resume in two ways. The simplest but least effective method is merely to list the job title you are seeking.

This approach is sufficient if you are using a chronological format and seeking the same job as your previous one—and if the entire emphasis of your resume is already on that job title and your accomplishments are in that area only.

EXAMPLE: SIMPLE OBJECTIVE

OBJECTIVE:	PHARMACIST

Use Your "Objective" as an Effective Marketing Tool!

One reason to add an objective into your resume is that it can be a means of marketing your unique combination of skills—both technical and interpersonal. Your objective is the first thing the reviewer reads, and you can use it to make a great first impression. The secret is to focus attention on those skills that are most valuable for the job and to add *one* major benefit you can offer the employer. You should view your objective as a "mini-resume," which summarizes why the employer should hire you.

An effective resume should be employer directed, as was explained in Chapter 2. Its main purpose is to inform an employer of what you can and will do for him or her. Displaying subjective skills in a resume can be tricky, since the major portion of a resume deals with previous employment, which does not lend itself to subjective analysis. One solution is to mention those skills in your objective. Here you may tell the employer something about yourself and your work ethic. You can add qualities such as "my attention to detail," "ability to delegate," or any other *subjective* statement that puts you in a favorable light—right from the start of your resume.

You can also summarize the major contribution and benefit you will offer; for example, hiring you will result in "increased sales," "a more efficiently run department," and so forth.

In short, an effectively written objective allows you to make a *personal statement* in your resume. It gives you the chance to tell employers up front what you can do for them and what benefits they will have by hiring you. Let us look at each step.

JOB TITLE

First, list the job title, as in a simple objective.

SKILLS YOU BRING TO THE JOB

Next, list your two or three top qualifications for the job. If you have many years of experience, you may want to list the number. If you have an outstanding accomplishment or unique combination of skills, you may mention that too. Additionally, adding one major personality trait that supports your objective is advantageous here.

EMPLOYER BENEFITS/RESULTS

Here you briefly state the employer's benefit of hiring you. That benefit can be: increased sales, greater market shares, development of new products, or even increased efficiency. These are all benefits that every employer desires.

EXAMPLE: **EFFECTIVE OBJECTIVE**

OBJECTIVE:	**PHARMACIST**—where my nine years of experience, my expertise in generic medications, and my ability to fill orders quickly will result in increased efficiency.

W O R K S H E E T   I N S T R U C T I O N S

Follow the instructions below to write your objective—one section at a time.

You will write

- ↷ your job title.
- ↷ the skills and experience you bring to the job, including an outstanding personality trait important for your career.
- ↷ the main benefit you offer the employer.

When you have finished, you will compose your final version, as you want it to appear on your resume, at the end of this section.

WRITING AN EFFECTIVE OBJECTIVE

Use your Skill Inventory Worksheet (Chapter 1) to assist you.

1. Job Title

Be specific. If you are seeking a job similar to one you have held in the past, that job title will be among those listed in your personal Skill Inventory Worksheet under Technical Skills.

If you are seeking a job in a new area, look at the list in Chapter 1 for examples of job titles. If the job you are seeking is from the want ads, tailor your job title to the one that appears in the ad.

> IF YOU ARE LOOKING FOR MULTIPLE JOBS IN DIVERSE AREAS, WRITE TWO RESUMES, EACH TAILORED SPECIFICALLY FOR EACH JOB.

2. Skills and Experience

What skills and experience can you bring to the position? Look at your list of skills in Chapter 1. Which of your general skills or, better yet, specific tasks will most impress the employer?

For example (a general skill and a specific task):

CUSTOMER SERVICE—where my communication skills and my ability to handle customer complaints will result in . . .

Or you may want to list your total years of experience:

CUSTOMER SERVICE—where my ten years of experience in customer service will be utilized to . . .

> **TWO IMPORTANT GUIDELINES:**
>
> 1. MAKE SURE EACH TASK OR SKILL AREA THAT YOU MENTION IS RELEVANT TO YOUR OBJECTIVE. IN OTHER WORDS, IF YOU ARE SEEKING A JOB AS AN ACCOUNTANT, YOUR CARPENTRY SKILLS WILL NOT MATTER TO YOUR EMPLOYER. WHAT MATTERS WILL BE YOUR ABILITY TO AUDIT FINANCIAL RECORDS AND YOUR TOTAL YEARS OF ACCOUNTING EXPERIENCE.
> 2. MAKE SURE YOUR RESUME SUPPORTS THE SKILLS YOU MENTION IN YOUR OBJECTIVE.

Look at your Skill Inventory Worksheet. Choose your two most impressive qualifications that relate to your career objective. Two major skill areas is acceptable. Alternatively, one skill area combined with one specific job task or your total years of experience in the field is also suitable. Choose two qualifications at maximum. Do not overdo it, but do not underplay it either.

Have you omitted any skill areas from your list? If so, add them to your list in Chapter 1 now.

From your Inventory Skill Worksheet in Chapter 1, fill in any two of the blanks in Item 2 of the practice worksheet.

3. Personality Trait

Which one of your self-management skills would most impress the employer? Be sure it relates to your job objective.

A personality trait is not something you must put into your objective. However, since this is the only place in your resume that you can make a subjective comment about yourself, the objective affords you the opportunity to make a statement such as "I work well under pressure," "I am a team player," and so forth.

You may want to check the list in Chapter 1 again for assistance.

4. Employer Benefits

What benefits can you offer the employer? On the practice worksheet is a chart of benefits that most employers look for. Look at the chart, and check the most important benefit you can offer. If the benefit you plan to bring to the job is not listed, write it yourself under the heading Other.

Make sure the benefit you check is one that you can realistically bring to the job and that the benefit follows logically from the skills you mention in your resume.

5. Putting It All Together

Use the following example as a guide to organize your information.

EXAMPLE: OBJECTIVE

> **OBJECTIVE:** **PERSONNEL MANAGEMENT**—where my five years management experience, my proven record in recruiting and training new workers, and my ability to motivate others will result in improved employee performance.

CHAPTER 5 **W O R K S H E E T**

Career Objective Practice

1. JOB TITLE: _____

2. MAJOR SKILL AREAS IMPORTANT FOR THE JOB:

1. _____

2. _____

SPECIFIC TASKS/ACCOMPLISHMENTS NEEDED FOR THE JOB:

1. _____

2. _____

NUMBER OF YEARS EXPERIENCE IN DESIRED FIELD: _____
(Add this *only* if you have an impressive number.)

3. MOST IMPORTANT PERSONALITY TRAIT NEEDED FOR THE JOB:

_____

4. CHECK THE MAIN BENEFIT(S) YOU WILL BRING TO THE JOB:

- ☐ Increase sales
- ☐ Increase market share
- ☐ Improve efficiency
- ☐ Develop new products
- ☐ Attract new clients

- ☐ Improve system performance
- ☐ Improve employee work performance
- ☐ Promote good customer relations
- ☐ Create new programs
- ☐ OTHER: _____

(continued)

CHAPTER 5 / WORKSHEET (continued)

Career Objective Practice

5. PUTTING IT ALL TOGETHER
Transfer your information from the previous page to the chart below:

_____
(job title)

where my _____
(skill #1 or years of experience)

_____
(skill #2)

_____
(personality trait—if applicable)

will result in _____
(benefit)

WORKSHEET INSTRUCTIONS

Compare the objective you wrote with the example at the bottom of page 24 and the previous example of the pharmacist on page 23.

Make whatever changes you need so that your objective flows smoothly.

Copy the final version of your objective on the worksheet page that follows.

Remember: write it *exactly* as you want it to appear on your resume.

RESUME STYLE GUIDLINES

Your job title should stand out. To do this use either caps, italics, boldface, underlining, or a combination. The choice is yours.

Instruct the typist how you want your job title printed.

EVEN IF YOUR RESUME DOES NOT WARRANT A LENGTHY OBJECTIVE, DO NOT OMIT IT ALTOGETHER. AT THE VERY LEAST, LIST THE JOB TITLE OF THE POSITION YOU ARE SEEKING (LIKE THE EXAMPLE OF THE PHARMACIST).

REMEMBER: AN *EFFECTIVE OBJECTIVE,* ONE THAT MENTIONS SKILLS AND BENEFITS, WILL BE TAKEN THE MOST SERIOUSLY.

CHAPTER 5

WORKSHEET

Career Objective

Career Objective:

_____

_____

_____

_____

_____

_____

_____

_____

_____

_____

Resume Style Guidelines:

Job title should be: ☐ CAPS ☐ **Bold** ☐ _Italics_ ☐ Underlined

SUMMARY OF QUALIFICATIONS

Short statements that highlight your most impressive qualifications and achievements

- The purpose of the summary is to immediately grab the employers' attention and impress them. It can be customized to fit the job you are pursuing.
- An effective summary will generate serious attention.
- To be effective, the statements must be concise, written with impact (action verbs), and result oriented.

WHEN TO INCLUDE AND WHEN TO OMIT A SUMMARY

The Summary of Qualifications or Highlight of Qualifications section is optional. Although an employer will not be disappointed if you omit it, when presented properly, this short summary can be a highly effective tool. By shining the spotlight on your most impressive achievements at the outset, you will grab the employer's attention immediately, and your resume will be read with heightened interest.

If you have a limited number of skills and achievements and you have already mentioned them in the objective, omitting the summary may be best. Mentioning the same skills repeatedly is overkill. Your resume will appear inflated, which may seriously damage your chances. On the other hand, if you are worried that an employer will overlook your impressive list of achievements if you bury them in the body of your resume, incorporating them in a summary is a good idea.

This rule applies particularly if you are using a chronological format, which focuses on job titles and dates of employment rather than skill areas. In such a case, highlighting your skill areas within the summary is wise.

Let employers know immediately who you are. Arouse their interest and make them want to finish reading your resume. The better the impression you make, the better your chances for an interview.

If you choose to include a Summary of Qualifications, be sure you write it with impact. If written poorly, the summary will backfire. The employer will be annoyed and may refuse to finish your resume. If you include a summary, do it right!

HOW TO WRITE AN EFFECTIVE SUMMARY

Select the Most Impressive Information

The Summary of Qualifications is a miniature resume. It focuses on the most important commodity you have to offer: your skills and accomplishments. You have one chance to grab the employer's attention, so you better make it count. Thus, writing your Summary of Qualifications with impact is crucial.

Your summary is similar to an advertisement. It announces what you have to offer. As with an ad, each statement must be concise, full of punch, and impressive.

What statements in an ad grab your attention? Those that solve a problem. Consider, as an example, these ads for a leading detergent: "Our detergent will cut your washing costs by 50 percent! Ours gets out even the most stubborn stains." Notice how these statements succinctly sell benefits.

You must do the same in your resume. You must sell yourself. Below is a list of ways to make your Summary of Qualifications sell you.

- ↷ List your most impressive qualifications—those that will be used to solve problems for your employer.

- ↷ List your most important accomplishments—problems that you have solved or results that you were directly responsible for in your past work experience.

- ↷ List personal qualities that would impress an employer—those that will grab the employer's attention, such as "more than 15 years of experience," "ability to work well under pressure," "scored 97 percent on Managers' Training Test."

Write with Impact

Going back to our detergent example, what do these statements have in common that catch our attention? They make claims that are result oriented. The ad tells us specifically how much we will save. The more detailed the statement, the more serious we take it.

The same is true in your resume. Be specific. Do not make general statements such as "I saved the company money" or "I increased efficiency." Give details. Write "I saved the company $4,000 in overhead," or "I increased efficiency by delegating more responsibility to staff members." The details add impact.

The second important principle is to write result-oriented statements. The previous examples give results: how much money was saved, how efficiency was increased. Focus on problems you have solved for previous employers or proven results that you were responsible for achieving. Employers are interested in results.

CAUTION: **Be careful not to overdo it. Limiting your summary to a maximum of six statements is best.**

Use Action Verbs

Always use action verbs to describe your accomplishments. Chapters 7 and 8 discuss in detail the proper use of action verbs.

Because most of your summary's content will be a digest of your experience and accomplishments, you should write it last. First, complete the upcoming sections. However, before continuing, consider the following examples. They will give you an idea of an effective Summary of Qualifications. Return and write your Summary of Qualifications after you have finished the rest of your resume.

EXAMPLE: **A SUMMARY FOR A MANAGER**

SUMMARY OF QUALIFICATIONS	
	• Hired and trained 24 assistant managers in one year
	• Created successful questionnaire for evaluating work activities of personnel
	• Supervised turnover reduction of more than 60 percent
	• Received "Manager of the Year Award" 1991
	• Ability to handle pressure and complete the job on time

WHAT ARE THE KEY ELEMENTS OF THIS SUMMARY?

↪ EACH STATEMENT IS CONCISE, DIRECT, AND RESULT ORIENTED.

↪ ACTION VERBS (HIRED, TRAINED, CREATED, AND EVALUATED) ADD IMPACT.

↪ MENTIONING THE AWARD IN THE SUMMARY ENSURES THAT THE EMPLOYER WILL READ IT.

↪ ADDING THE PERSONAL QUALITY OF BEING ABLE TO HANDLE PRESSURE, A SITUATION EVERY MANAGER MUST FACE, ADDS AMPLE REINFORCEMENT.

EXAMPLE: **A SUMMARY FOR A SECRETARY**

SUMMARY OF QUALIFICATIONS	
	• More than 15 years experience
	• Proficient in WordPerfect and Microsoft Word
	• Evaluated office supply vendors for best price and reduced purchasing costs by 10 percent
	• Knowledge of light bookkeeping and payroll
	• Highly motivated team player

WHAT IS AN EMPLOYER LOOKING FOR IN A SECRETARY?

↪ EXPERIENCE—IF A PERSON HAS WORKED FIVE OR TEN YEARS AS A SECRETARY, HE OR SHE KNOWS HOW TO TYPE, TRANSCRIBE DICTATION, AND FILE. HERE EXPERIENCE IS A DEFINITE EDGE OVER THE COMPETITION.

↪ FAMILIARITY WITH WORD PROCESSING PROGRAMS—IN PARTICULAR, WORDPERFECT AND MICROSOFT WORD, THE TWO LEADING WORD PROCESSING PROGRAMS IN USE.

↪ BOOKKEEPING AND PAYROLL SKILLS—MANY SECRETARIES LACK THESE ABILITIES. MENTIONING THEM GIVES YOU AN ADVANTAGE.

When done effectively, the summary will give employers a positive image of you. It will impress them and entice them to read more. Be sure that the body of your resume supports and enhances what you have written in your objective and summary of qualifications.

CAUTION: **Although the "summary of qualifications" is one of the first sections appearing on your resume, you will write it last. It is a "summary" of your resume, and therefore, you should write it after you have finished your resume—when you can select your most impressive qualifications from the body of your resume.**

Do not complete the following worksheet until you have finished the following chapters:

↷ Chapters 7 and 8, Professional Experience

↷ Chapter 9, Education

↷ Chapter 10, Additional Qualifications

W O R K S H E E T   I N S T R U C T I O N S

If your resume warrants a Summary of Qualifications (most do), select five or six (never more than six at the most) of your most outstanding qualifications.

Select this information from your:

1. Unique skills or combination of skills in your Skill List (Chapter 1).

2. List of achievements in your Professional Experience section (Chapter 7 or 8).

3. Outstanding educational achievements in your Education section (Chapter 9).

4. Special awards, honors, or special training (Chapter 10).

5. Total years of experience in the field (only if it is an impressive number).

6. Outstanding personality traits in your Skill List (Chapter 1).

↷ Write each statement with punch—concise and directly to the point.

↷ Make sure your statements are result oriented.

↷ Use action verbs to describe your achievements.

↷ Reread the section on action verbs in Chapters 7 and 8.

Copy your summary, *exactly* as you want it to appear on your resume, on the worksheet page that follows.

RESUME STYLE GUIDELINES

Highlight each statement of your summary with a bullet. In the examples on the previous pages, notice how the bullet (•) made each statement stand out. You can also use a check (✔), an em-dash (—), or whatever symbol you want. The purpose is to distinguish your summary.

Instruct the typist how you want your statements bulleted.

CHAPTER 6 · WORKSHEET

Summary of Qualifications

Summary of Qualifications:

1. _____

_____

2. _____

_____

3. _____

_____

4. _____

_____

5. _____

_____

6. _____

_____

Resume Style Guidelines:

Each statement should be highlighted with a: ☐ • ☐ ✓ ☐ Other: _____

PROFESSIONAL EXPERIENCE— CHRONOLOGICAL

A summary of your employment history

In a Chronological Resume this includes:

- dates of employment (month, year)
- name of the company or organization you worked for
- description of the organization (if necessary)
- location of the company (city and state)
- job title(s)
- responsibilities and duties
- accomplishments, results of these accomplishments, and demonstrated skills

List all past employment, beginning with your most recent employer. Document your work experience by listing your duties and tasks. Demonstrate your ability to contribute by emphasizing your accomplishments and skills.

YOUR PROFESSIONAL EXPERIENCE IS THE HEART OF YOUR RESUME

This section of your resume is the most widely and carefully read by employers. They will meticulously inspect it to find reasons for eliminating you. Do not give them any cause for alarm. Eliminate negative references. Accentuate only positive qualifications and accomplishments.

Demonstrate that you have the experience and the ability to do the job. Prove that you are someone who can solve problems and contribute significantly.

However, do not overdo it. Be selective. Choose only enough relevant information to create a positive image and to make the employer curious enough to want to meet you in person in an interview.

Be sure to present the information in an eye-catching layout. Do not lump everything together in one paragraph, because the employer must be able to quickly scan it and gain a thorough picture of you and your accomplishments.

Make your job titles stand out by using boldface type or underlining them. Additionally, emphasize the name of past companies by using caps or underlining. Accomplishments should be concise and bulleted.

HOW TO PRESENT YOUR INFORMATION

Dates of Employment

↪ Employers expect to see your dates of employment, and may check your resume for time gaps. List both month and year you began working and the month and year your employment was terminated (or write "until present" if you are still working at the job). If you indicate only the years, employers may suspect a gap. Conversely, listing more than the month is unnecessary. Short gaps of a few weeks or one month are expected.

↪ If you have gaps and you want to camouflage them, you have two choices. You can list your dates of employment after you have listed the company's name and location. (See the Example on page 46.) Listing it at the end detracts attention. Alternatively, you may choose to list *only* the years of employment. Although this is a poor proposition (as stated earlier), resort to it if you have no choice.

↪ If you held many part-time jobs and do not want to look like a "jobhopper" (a symbol of instability), consolidate them into one heading such as: 1994–Present: Part-time Employment; or even better: Consultant.

Company's Name, Description, and Location

↪ List the company name. If it is a large corporation, you may want to add the division in which you worked. For example: AT&T—Computer Division. If the company is a subsidiary of a larger, more prestigious corporation, add that in your resume. For example: Films Classics, Inc., a division of Paramount Pictures Corporation.

↪ If your past employer is not well known (or is not local), you should write a one-line description of the company so that future employers will get an idea of the type and size of the corporation for which you have worked. For example: Metro Group, a local retail clothing chain with yearly sales in excess of $2 million. Managing a local chain store is significantly different than managing a small "Mom-and-Pop" outfit. An employer understands the level of your responsibilities by understanding the type of organizations for which you have worked. The same rule is true for a division. Add a line of description about your division if it is vague.

↪ List the city and state where your past employer is located. Do not mention street addresses or phone numbers. If needed, the employer can obtain that information or request it on a job application.

Job Title

↪ Use a generic job title, one that every employer understands. Avoid such titles as Jr. Data Entry Operator—Level Two. It will probably mean little to anyone outside your former organization. Simply state, Data Entry Operator.

↪ Choose a job title that reflects your level of responsibility. If you were a secretary who was actively involved in decision making, you may want to represent your job title as Administrative Assistant rather than Secretary.

CAUTION: **If you do this, be sure your past employer will support you. If someone checks on you and your former boss tells them you were a Secretary and not an Assistant, you could jeopardize your chances of getting the job. Be sure to check creative job titles with former employers before using them on your resume.**

↪ If you have had more than one job title at the same company (you have been promoted), set off each job title. List your total years at the company and the company name at the top. Under it, list each job title separately. Under each job title, list the duties and accomplishments for it. Emphasize upward mobility and increased responsibility with each job.

Duties and Responsibilities

↱ List three or four of your major duties. Precede it with a catchall phrase such as Duties included . . . , or Responsible for . . . . Always use action verbs.

↱ Mention the people (by job title, not name) you interacted with on the job. For example: Reported to Vice President of Sales, or Supervised Four Account Executives.

↱ Do not repeat your responsibilities. If you have had more than one job with similar duties, mention those duties only once. If you did dictation in one job, you should not repeat that information again about another job. The reader already knows you have that skill.

↱ Always show upward mobility. Detail your less important duties on earlier jobs and reserve your most impressive duties for your most recent job.

Accomplishments

↱ List your most impressive accomplishments first. Be specific. Qualify your accomplishments in terms of money saved or other concrete employer benefits. Emphasize the skills you applied and use action verbs.

↱ Do not tell *how* you achieved your accomplishments. Make the employer interested enough to discover how you did it during an interview.

EXAMPLE: **YEARS ARE EMPHASIZED**

PROFESSIONAL EXPERIENCE:

Feb. 2000 to Present

McNAIR MANUFACTURING, INC., Chicago, IL
Shoe manufacturer employing 200+ employees
Gross sales for 2002 exceeded $2 million.

MANAGER
Responsibilities included supervising staff of 12, coordinating advertising and promotions, training new employees. Reported directly to CEO.
• Reduced annual operating costs 5 percent by improving warehouse procedure.
• Restructured employee communications program, increasing in-house communications efficiency.

ASSISTANT MANAGER
In charge of developing employee training programs
• Awarded Employee of the Year Award, 2004

March 1999 to Jan. 2000

MAY COMPANY—SHOE DEPARTMENT, Chicago, IL

MANAGER
Assisted sales staff in developing more effective sales techniques; oversaw all aspects of the department, including inventory and apprised Senior Management of weekly business activity.
• Under my leadership, department sales increased more than 18 percent.

EXAMPLE: **YEARS ARE NOT EMPHASIZED**

EXPERIENCE:	Marketing Group, Chicago, IL 2004 to Present

ACCOUNT EXECUTIVE
Responsible for initiating new advertising accounts
- Acquired a major account (Calco, Inc.) resulting in 12% revenue increase
- Conceived of and authored Monthly Newsletter to raise clients' awareness of new company services

Whitmer Advertising, Chicago, IL 2001 to 2004

JR. ACCOUNT EXECUTIVE
Was introduced to all aspects of advertising, including TV and radio sales, print ads, and public relations.

WHAT IF YOU HAVE NO OUTSTANDING ACCOMPLISHMENTS?

If you do not have any outstanding accomplishments, then stress your skills. For example, if you have been driving a truck for the last six years, even though you did not achieve anything significant, you still have qualifications you can emphasize; namely, your unique *combination* of skills.

Which of your skills are *unique*? As a truck driver, perhaps you have an outstanding driving record. Maybe you have a thorough knowledge of the state's or nation's highways. Whatever job or training you have, you can find unique skills that you have acquired and present yourself with impact.

EXAMPLE: **SKILLS ARE EMPHASIZED**

EXPERIENCE:

2005 to Present: Chicago Metro Delivery, Chicago, IL

DRIVER
- Freight transportation in Chicago area
- Inventory control
- Thoroughly familiar with Chicago and environs
- Impeccable driving record

You can also use your Summary of Qualifications to emphasize skills. Skills such as "your impeccable driving record" or "your familiarity with the Chicago region," could also be listed in your Summary. However, do not list them twice. If you list them in your Summary, do not list them again in your Professional Experience. Mentioning the same facts repeatedly, or resorting to puffery, will only hurt your chances.

Any of your outstanding character or personality traits that are crucial for the job you seek can also be listed in your Summary. In the previous example, adding a trait such as "dependable and hard working" would enhance the resume.

The essential goal is to present yourself with impact and show that you are someone who takes action and gets things done. Thus, even if you do not have any outstanding achievements, you can still emphasize your skills in your Summary of Qualifications and Experience sections.

You will now proceed to write your Professional Experience. First, we will explain how to bring your resume to life using action verbs. Remember this is the heart of your resume, so take your time, study the action verbs, and give it your all.

ACTION VERBS

What Are Action Verbs and Why Must You Use Them?

Action verbs conjure up a positive image in the reader's mind. They demonstrate action and results. They are concise and focused, and they enliven a resume.

For example, assume you started a new program to train employees. You could simply state, in very dull terms: "Started a new program to train employees." Or you could state the same information with impact: "Initiated an employee-training program." Notice the difference. The term "initiated" is active and focused. Other suitable action terms here are "created and implemented" or "developed." These words emphasize action—action on your part to get the job done.

However, this example still lacks something. It lacks results. Why does your new program matter? What did it accomplish for your employer?

Whenever possible, connect action verbs with results. If the results of your new program were that employees were trained in three days instead of four, you could write: "Initiated new employee-training program that cut training time 25 percent." Another example is if one of your duties was to purchase office supplies. You could simply state the facts: "In charge of purchasing office supplies." However, a more effective way to present yourself would be to highlight the skills you used. You probably searched for the best price and may have even negotiated for lower prices. If so, write with impact: "Evaluated vendors and negotiated for the best prices on all office supplies." The benefit to the employer (the fact that you got the best price, which saved him or her money) is obvious.

Use action verbs anytime you describe your duties, accomplishments, or qualifications.

Which Action Verbs Best Describe *Your* Accomplishments?

The following list will help you find the right action verbs to describe your accomplishments. The key verbs are sorted according to skill areas. If your job was one that required "managerial skills," the action verbs that describe your task(s) will likely be under that heading.

Most jobs require a combination of skills. Check *all* skill areas that apply to you. Record verbs that could qualify and describe your duties and accomplishments.

Often, multiple words are serviceable. For example, if your job required you to write reports, you could choose any of the following action verbs: wrote, authored, compiled, composed, edited, organized, or designed. They are all effective. Deciding which best describes your accomplishments is your preference.

Action Verbs Are the Key to an Effective Resume Because They

- create impact and enliven a resume.
- emphasize action and accomplishments.
- present you as an "achiever" and a "success."
- concisely focus the reader's attention on your accomplishments.

Action Verbs—Categorized by Skill Areas

Creative

authored
conceived
created
designed
developed
devised
directed
enhanced
established
formulated
illustrated
improved
initiated
introduced
invented
launched
marketed
originated
planned
prepared
produced
proposed
set up
structured
wrote

Clerical and Research

arranged
automated
budgeted
calculated
catalogued
classified
collected
compared
compiled
completed
computed
critiqued
decreased
diagnosed
dispatched
distributed
evaluated
examined
executed
generated
identified
implemented
inspected
interpreted
interviewed
investigated
monitored
operated
organized
prepared
processed
purchased
recorded
retrieved
reviewed
scheduled
screened
summarized
surveyed
systematized
tabulated
validated
verified

Human Resources

advised
assessed
assisted
clarified
coached
collaborated
consulted
counseled
diagnosed
educated
employed
grouped
guided
handled
hired
integrated
mediated
monitored
motivated
negotiated
recruited
represented
sponsored
strengthened
trained

Management and Leadership

administered
analyzed

assigned
attained
authorized
chaired
consolidated
contracted
controlled
coordinated
delegated
developed
directed
enacted
established
evaluated
exceeded
executed
expanded
guided
headed
implemented
improved
incorporated
increased
initiated
instituted
investigated
launched
led
maintained
managed
mediated
negotiated
organized
oversaw
performed
planned
prioritized
produced
proposed
recommended
reduced
repositioned
retained
reviewed
revised
scheduled
sorted
strengthened
supervised

Technical

assembled
built

calculated
computed
designed
engineered
operated
overhauled
programmed
remodeled
repaired
solved
upgraded

Financial

allocated
analyzed
appraised
audited
balanced
budgeted
calculated
computed
forecasted
managed
marketed
planned
projected
tabulated

Teaching

advised
clarified
coached
communicated
encouraged
evaluated
explained
guided
influenced
informed
instructed
interpreted
lectured
persuaded
stimulated
trained

Communication

addressed
arbitrated
arranged

Success Words

authored
convinced
corresponded
developed
directed
drafted
edited
enlisted
formulated
influenced
interpreted
interviewed
lectured
moderated
negotiated
participated
persuaded
presented
presided
promoted
publicized
recruited
represented
sold
spoke
translated
wrote

accomplished
awarded
corrected
diverted
eliminated
expanded
generated
identified
improved
masterminded
pioneered
rectified
solved
strengthened
surpassed
turned around
was promoted to
was responsible for

W O R K S H E E T   I N S T R U C T I O N S

JOB TITLE

On the following worksheet pages, you will write your work experience. On the first page, list your most recent job. On the following pages, list any prior jobs, always mentioning your more recent employment first. (Four worksheets have been provided. If you need more, you may duplicate the worksheet for your use.)

If you have held multiple jobs at the same company:

Devote a separate page to each job title. List the total years you have worked for that company on the first page. On the remaining worksheets, leave this information blank. However, make a notation for the typist "same as previous page" so that when you type your resume, you or your typist will understand that all the job titles should be under the same employer heading.

If you have held more than four jobs:

Add extra pages, and follow the same format. Preferably, limit your work experience to four jobs. If you have held many jobs in a short span of time, you will look like a job-hopper (a sign of instability). Consolidate those jobs into one title such as: Part-time Employment or Consultant, or list only your last four jobs.

DUTIES

What did you do on a daily basis? List your most important tasks first. Use action verbs and stress your skills. Indicate your level of responsibility, such as who you reported to and how many employees you managed. *Above all, be concise!* Do not list more than four duties.

ACCOMPLISHMENTS

Mention important projects on which you worked. Stress your contribution. What compliments did you receive from your boss or coworkers? What have you done that improved the company or saved it money? These are all guidelines for analyzing your accomplishments.

Emphasize all accomplishments in terms of benefits to the employer.

Benefits include:

- Saving money
- Increasing profits
- Lowering unit costs
- Solving emergency situations
- Streamlining operations
- Improving employee relations
- Decreasing costs
- Increasing efficiency
- Eliminating waste
- Expanding client base
- Introducing a new product
- Improving working conditions

Be specific. Give numbers and percentages if possible.

If you made no *major* contributions, stress your skills and skill areas.

RESUME STYLE GUIDELINES

Use bullets for emphasis to distinguish your list of duties and accomplishments.

CHAPTER 7 **WORKSHEET**

Professional Experience—Chronological

BE SURE TO FILL OUT *BOTH SIDES* OF THIS SHEET.

Professional Experience:

JOB TITLE—MOST RECENT JOB:

_____

DATE EMPLOYMENT BEGAN (Month, Year):   DATE TERMINATED (or "to Present"):

_____, 20_____   _____

NAME OF EMPLOYER/COMPANY/ORGANIZATION AND DEPARTMENT (if company is large):

_____

EMPLOYER'S ADDRESS (City, State):

_____

_____

_____

DESCRIPTION OF THE COMPANY OR DEPARTMENT (if the company is not well-known):

_____

_____

_____

(continued)

Professional Experience—Chronological

DUTIES AND RESPONSIBILITIES:

List three or four of your daily tasks and duties.

(Begin with the catchphrase: "Responsible for/Responsibilities included/Duties included." Bullet [•] each "duty" for emphasis.)

_____

_____

_____

_____

_____

_____

ACCOMPLISHMENTS OR MAJOR SKILLS:

List four or five. Bullet [•] each for emphasis.

_____

_____

_____

_____

_____

_____

_____

_____

CHAPTER 7   WORKSHEET

Professional Experience—Chronological

BE SURE TO FILL OUT *BOTH SIDES* OF THIS SHEET.

Professional Experience:

JOB TITLE—MOST RECENT JOB:

_____

DATE EMPLOYMENT BEGAN (Month, Year):   DATE TERMINATED (or "to Present"):

_____, 20_____   _____

NAME OF EMPLOYER/COMPANY/ORGANIZATION AND DEPARTMENT (if company is large):

_____

EMPLOYER'S ADDRESS (City, State):

_____

_____

_____

DESCRIPTION OF THE COMPANY OR DEPARTMENT (if the company is not well-known):

_____

_____

_____

(continued)

CHAPTER 7   WORKSHEET (continued)

Professional Experience— Chronological

DUTIES AND RESPONSIBILITIES:

List three or four of your daily tasks and duties.

(Begin with the catchphrase: "Responsible for/Responsibilities included/Duties included." Bullet [•] each "duty" for emphasis.)

_____

_____

_____

_____

_____

_____

_____

ACCOMPLISHMENTS OR MAJOR SKILLS:

List four or five. Bullet [•] each for emphasis.

_____

_____

_____

_____

_____

_____

_____

_____

CHAPTER 7 / **W O R K S H E E T**

Professional Experience— Chronological

BE SURE TO FILL OUT *BOTH SIDES* OF THIS SHEET.

Professional Experience:

JOB TITLE—MOST RECENT JOB:

_____

DATE EMPLOYMENT BEGAN (Month, Year):   DATE TERMINATED (or "to Present"):

_____, 20_____   _____

NAME OF EMPLOYER/COMPANY/ORGANIZATION AND DEPARTMENT (if company is large):

_____

EMPLOYER'S ADDRESS (City, State):

_____

_____

_____

DESCRIPTION OF THE COMPANY OR DEPARTMENT (if the company is not well-known):

_____

_____

_____

(continued)

Professional Experience—
Chronological

DUTIES AND RESPONSIBILITIES:

List three or four of your daily tasks and duties.

(Begin with the catchphrase: "Responsible for/Responsibilities included/Duties included." Bullet [•] each "duty" for emphasis.)

_____

_____

_____

_____

_____

_____

_____

ACCOMPLISHMENTS OR MAJOR SKILLS:

List four or five. Bullet [•] each for emphasis.

_____

_____

_____

_____

_____

_____

_____

_____

CHAPTER 7   **WORKSHEET**

Professional Experience— Chronological

BE SURE TO FILL OUT *BOTH SIDES* OF THIS SHEET.

Professional Experience:

JOB TITLE—MOST RECENT JOB:

_____

DATE EMPLOYMENT BEGAN (Month, Year):   DATE TERMINATED (or "to Present"):

_____, 20_____   _____

NAME OF EMPLOYER/COMPANY/ORGANIZATION AND DEPARTMENT (if company is large):

_____

EMPLOYER'S ADDRESS (City, State):

_____

_____

_____

DESCRIPTION OF THE COMPANY OR DEPARTMENT (if the company is not well-known):

_____

_____

_____

(continued)

CHAPTER 7   **W O R K S H E E T** (continued)

Professional Experience— Chronological

DUTIES AND RESPONSIBILITIES:

List three or four of your daily tasks and duties.

(Begin with the catchphrase: "Responsible for/Responsibilities included/Duties included." Bullet [•] each "duty" for emphasis.)

_____

_____

_____

_____

_____

_____

ACCOMPLISHMENTS OR MAJOR SKILLS:

List four or five. Bullet [•] each for emphasis.

_____

_____

_____

_____

_____

_____

_____

PROFESSIONAL EXPERIENCE– FUNCTIONAL

A summary of your skill areas and employment history

In a Functional Resume this includes:

- headings that emphasize skill areas.
- job responsibilities, duties, and accomplishments organized according to the skills they utilize.
- skills and accomplishments primarily emphasized over job titles or periods of employment.

In a Hybrid Resume you would also include:

- a list of employers and job titles, and optionally, dates of employment.

EMPHASIZE YOUR SKILLS

As previously mentioned, the functional resume is particularly effective if you have limited experience in the workplace or if you are changing jobs. The functional format will focus the employer's attention on your skills rather than your limited experience or, if you have continuously changed jobs, your excessively numerous employers.

LIST YOUR DUTIES AND STRESS YOUR ACCOMPLISHMENTS

In the functional resume you also list your work experience (your duties and accomplishments), just as you do in the chronological resume. The difference is in the presentation. In the chronological format, everything is organized chronologically and listed according to the job title and employer. In a functional format, all similar qualifications are organized under the same skill heading, regardless of where or when they were performed.

For example, if you worked for McCormick Public Relations and were in charge of print ads for two years and then took a job with another agency and were in charge of print ads and radio for three years, you would list all of these skills under one heading. You might use the headline Advertising and under it list all of your advertising experience.

In this case, it would include: "More than five years of print ad experience. Demonstrated ability to coordinate print and radio advertising" and so forth. If you also did clerical work while at McCormick, you would list that under another headline— Clerical or perhaps Administrative Skills.

BE CONCISE

This rule holds true regardless of whatever format you choose. Limit your skill headings to three at maximum. If you have more, consolidate them. For example, you could combine Advertising and Public Relations into one heading.

Choose only those skill headings that support your objective. If you are looking for a job as an accountant, you would want to use headings such as Accounting or Budgeting, rather than Teaching or Motivational Training. Remember be selective and choose *only* skill areas that interest your employer. Eliminate everything else.

Never mention information repeatedly, and always focus attention particularly on those accomplishments that resulted in tangible benefits for the employer.

THE HYBRID RESUME

One of the best features of the functional resume is that it lets you choose which skills you want to emphasize. The main problem with this format is that many employers worry that you are exaggerating your skills or, worse, you are hiding something. Moreover, employers want to see the names of your past employers. Knowing the type of organization you have worked for helps them understand the responsibilities you can handle, as well as the quality of the work they can expect from you.

Therefore, in the hybrid resume, you present a Short Summary of your past employers. You list your job title, as well as the name and location of your previous employment. If you have a solid history, you should mention the dates of employment as well. However, you do not mention your duties or accomplishments, because you have already listed them under your skill areas.

The following example is for someone whose objective is Sales. Note how only sales-related skill headings are used. In a classic functional resume, the Employment History section would be omitted.

The following example is a hybrid format with employment history summarized.

Example: Hybrid Format

MARKETING & SALES
- Sold custom designed fixtures and standard display products
- Researched and developed target market and leads
- Expanded client base to include major corporations
- Organized local trade shows

PROMOTION & ADVERTISING
- Implemented promotional giveaway program that increased sales 12 percent
- Designed successful advertising materials
- Developed point-of-purchase displays for the company's six stores
- Researched and selected local trade publications to place ads with greatest cost efficiency

EMPLOYMENT HISTORY

Sales Manager
Jerry's Fixtures, St. Paul, MN—Largest fixtures chain in the St. Paul area

Salesman
Sunshine World, St. Paul, MN

ACTION VERBS

What Are Action Verbs and Why Must You Use Them?

Action verbs conjure up a positive image in the reader's mind. They demonstrate action and results. They are concise and focused, and they enliven a resume.

For example, assume you started a new program to train employees. You could simply state, in very dull terms: "Started a new program to train employees." Or you could state the same information with impact: "Initiated an employee-training program." Notice the difference. The term "initiated" is active and focused. Other suitable action terms here are "created and implemented" or "developed." These words emphasize action—action on your part to get the job done.

However, this example still lacks something. It lacks results. Why does your new program matter? What did it accomplish for your employer?

Whenever possible, connect action verbs with results. If the results of your new program were that employees were trained in three days instead of four, you could write: "Initiated new employee-training program that cut training time 25 percent."

Another example is if one of your duties was to purchase office supplies. You could simply state the facts: "In charge of purchasing office supplies." However, a more effective way to present yourself would be to highlight the skills you used. You probably searched for the best price and may have even negotiated for lower prices. If so, write with impact: "Evaluated vendors and negotiated for the best prices on all office supplies." The benefit to the employer (the fact that you got the best price, which saved him or her money) is obvious.

Use action verbs anytime you describe your duties, accomplishments, or qualifications.

Which Action Verbs Best Describe *Your* Accomplishments?

The following list will help you find the right action verbs to describe your accomplishments. The key verbs are sorted according to skill areas. If your job was one that required "managerial skills," the action verbs that describe your task(s) will likely be under that heading.

Most jobs require a combination of skills. Check *all* skill areas that apply to you. Record verbs that could qualify and describe your duties and accomplishments.

Often, multiple words are serviceable. For example, if your job required you to write reports, you could choose any of the following action verbs: wrote, authored, compiled, composed, edited, organized, or designed. They are all effective. Deciding which best describes your accomplishments is your preference.

> ### *Action Verbs Are the Key to an Effective Resume Because They*
>
> - create impact and enliven a resume.
> - emphasize action and accomplishments.
> - present you as an "achiever" and a "success."
> - concisely focus the reader's attention on your accomplishments.

Action Verbs—Categorized by Skill Areas

Creative

authored
conceived
created
designed
developed
devised
directed
enhanced
established
formulated
illustrated
improved
initiated
introduced
invented
launched
marketed
originated
planned
prepared
produced
proposed
set up
structured
wrote

Clerical and Research

arranged
automated
budgeted
calculated
catalogued
classified
collected
compared
compiled
completed
computed
critiqued
decreased
diagnosed
dispatched
distributed
evaluated
examined
executed
generated
identified
implemented
inspected
interpreted

interviewed
investigated
monitored
operated
organized
prepared
processed
purchased
recorded
retrieved
reviewed
scheduled
screened
summarized
surveyed
systematized
tabulated
validated
verified

Human Resources

advised
assessed
assisted
clarified
coached
collaborated
consulted
counseled
diagnosed
educated
employed
grouped
guided
handled
hired
integrated
mediated
monitored
motivated
negotiated
recruited
represented
sponsored
strengthened
trained

Management and Leadership

administered
analyzed

assigned
attained
authorized
chaired
consolidated
contracted
controlled
coordinated
delegated
developed
directed
enacted
established
evaluated
exceeded
executed
expanded
guided
headed
implemented
improved
incorporated
increased
initiated
instituted
investigated
launched
led
maintained
managed
mediated
negotiated
organized
oversaw
performed
planned
prioritized
produced
proposed
recommended
reduced
repositioned
retained
reviewed
revised
scheduled
sorted
strengthened
supervised

Technical

assembled
built

calculated
computed
designed
engineered
operated
overhauled
programmed
remodeled
repaired
solved
upgraded

Financial

allocated
analyzed
appraised
audited
balanced
budgeted
calculated
computed
forecasted
managed
marketed
planned
projected
tabulated

Teaching

advised
clarified
coached
communicated
encouraged
evaluated
explained
guided
influenced
informed
instructed
interpreted
lectured
persuaded
stimulated
trained

Communication

addressed
arbitrated
arranged

authored
convinced
corresponded
developed
directed
drafted
edited
enlisted
formulated
influenced
interpreted
interviewed
lectured
moderated
negotiated
participated
persuaded
presented
presided
promoted
publicized
recruited
represented
sold
spoke
translated
wrote

Success Words

accomplished
awarded
corrected
diverted
eliminated
expanded
generated
identified
improved
masterminded
pioneered
rectified
solved
strengthened
surpassed
turned around
was promoted to
was responsible for

W O R K S H E E T   I N S T R U C T I O N S

The following four practice worksheets should prepare you for writing a functional or hybrid resume.

The first step in writing a functional resume is to choose your Skill Headings. This can be complicated.

We usually think in concrete terms (what tasks we performed) rather than thinking in the abstract (what skills we utilized).

These practice worksheets should help you analyze which skills or skill areas you used most often.

On the practice worksheets, enter your employment history in chronological order, beginning with your last job. List your job title, employer, and dates of employment. If you choose a traditional functional format, this information will not appear in your resume. However, documenting it will focus you.

Next, list your three major duties and three major accomplishments for each job. Then, on the line to the right of each duty and accomplishment, list the skill or skills that you used for that job.

For example, if you kept books, took dictation, and did word processing, your list might look like this:

1.	Bookkeeping	Financial and Clerical Skills
2.	Dictation	Clerical Skills
3.	Word Processing	Computer and Clerical Skills

In this example, the tasks could all be listed together under one heading: CLERICAL. Alternatively, they could each be listed under separate headings: Bookkeeping under FINANCIAL, Dictation under CLERICAL, and Word Processing under COMPUTER. The choice is yours, and it will depend upon which major skill areas you want to emphasize.

Review the charts in Chapter 1, Skill Assessment. Items in the list of Technical Skills can be Skill Headings. The list of Skill Areas and Specific Tasks will also help.

After you have compiled a list from your last four jobs, check the skill areas you have listed. The ones that appear the most are your *major skill areas*.

From these major skills, which ones are the most relevant to the job you are presently seeking?

The skill areas that fulfill both requirements (major skill areas and those that are most relevant to your Career Objective) are the Skill Headings you will use in your resume. Choose the three most impressive headings.

There are three final worksheets for skill headings; you will devote one page to each skill heading.

Under each heading, list the three or four most impressive duties and accomplishments that you performed with that skill. Finding that information should be easy. Check the right-hand column for the skill, and then look at the task associated with it.

These worksheets enable you to compose quickly and accurately a functional-format resume.

If you want to use the hybrid format, add your list of job titles and employers (and optionally, your periods of employment) on the last worksheet page of this chapter under Employment History. That information should also be easy to find—copy it from the top portion of your worksheets.

If you have too many major skill areas, consolidate them. Combine two similar skills into one heading, such as Publicity and Advertising or Marketing and Sales. Additionally, if one task involves two skills (word processing involves both Computer Skills and Clerical Skills), choose the one that best corresponds with your career goal.

Use Action Verbs

Review the list on page 62 and use it as an aid in describing your duties and accomplishments.

CHAPTER 8   W O R K S H E E T

Professional Experience
Practice

JOB TITLE: _____

NAME OF EMPLOYER: _____

EMPLOYER'S CITY AND STATE: _____

DATES OF EMPLOYMENT (Month, Year):

From: _____ , 20_____ to _____ , 20_____

THREE MAJOR DUTIES OR RESPONSIBILITIES: **SKILLS USED:**

1. _____   _____

    _____   _____

2. _____   _____

    _____   _____

3. _____   _____

    _____   _____

THREE MAJOR ACCOMPLISHMENTS: **SKILLS USED:**

1. _____   _____

    _____   _____

2. _____   _____

    _____   _____

3. _____   _____

    _____   _____

CHAPTER 8   **WORKSHEET**

Professional Experience Practice

JOB TITLE: _____

NAME OF EMPLOYER: _____

EMPLOYER'S CITY AND STATE: _____

DATES OF EMPLOYMENT (Month, Year):

From: _____ , 20_____ to _____ , 20_____

THREE MAJOR DUTIES OR RESPONSIBILITIES: **SKILLS USED:**

1. _____   _____

   _____   _____

2. _____   _____

   _____   _____

3. _____   _____

   _____   _____

THREE MAJOR ACCOMPLISHMENTS: **SKILLS USED:**

1. _____   _____

   _____   _____

2. _____   _____

   _____   _____

3. _____   _____

   _____   _____

CHAPTER 8

WORKSHEET

Professional Experience Practice

JOB TITLE: _____

NAME OF EMPLOYER: _____

EMPLOYER'S CITY AND STATE: _____

DATES OF EMPLOYMENT (Month, Year):

From: _____ , 20_____ to _____ , 20_____

THREE MAJOR DUTIES OR RESPONSIBILITIES: **SKILLS USED:**

1. _____   _____

   _____   _____

2. _____   _____

   _____   _____

3. _____   _____

   _____   _____

THREE MAJOR ACCOMPLISHMENTS: **SKILLS USED:**

1. _____   _____

   _____   _____

2. _____   _____

   _____   _____

3. _____   _____

   _____   _____

CHAPTER 8   **WORKSHEET**

Professional Experience Practice

JOB TITLE: _____

NAME OF EMPLOYER: _____

EMPLOYER'S CITY AND STATE: _____

DATES OF EMPLOYMENT (Month, Year):

From: _____ , 20_____ to _____ , 20_____

THREE MAJOR DUTIES OR RESPONSIBILITIES: **SKILLS USED:**

1. _____   _____

   _____   _____

2. _____   _____

   _____   _____

3. _____   _____

   _____   _____

THREE MAJOR ACCOMPLISHMENTS: **SKILLS USED:**

1. _____   _____

   _____   _____

2. _____   _____

   _____   _____

3. _____   _____

   _____   _____

W O R K S H E E T   I N S T R U C T I O N S

Functional Format

Complete the following worksheet pages exactly as you want them to appear on your resume.

Fill in your Skill Heading at the top of each worksheet.

Under each Skill Heading, list four or five qualifications that fall under that particular skill.

Qualifications can be either duties and responsibilities or accomplishments. Limit yourself to five maximum.

You should also compare your worksheets with your Skill Sheet (Chapter 1). Additionally, reviewing the Skill Lists in Chapter 1 should help you avoid omitting an important skill.

↷ Use action verbs to describe your skills and accomplishments.
↷ Do not repeat information.
↷ Be concise.

Hybrid Format

Complete the last page, too. The heading is Employment History.

List your past job titles, employers, location of employment, and, if you have a solid work history, your time periods of employment.

RESUME STYLE GUIDELINES

Emphasize qualifications and duties with bullets before each statement.

CHAPTER 8

WORKSHEET

Professional Experience—Functional

Professional Experience:

Skill Heading _____

LIST FOUR OR FIVE MAJOR DUTIES AND/OR ACCOMPLISHMENTS:

(Use bullets in front of each statement.)

1. _____

   _____

   _____

2. _____

   _____

   _____

3. _____

   _____

   _____

4. _____

   _____

   _____

5. _____

   _____

   _____

   _____

CHAPTER 8 WORKSHEET

Professional Experience—Functional

Professional Experience:

Skill Heading _____

LIST FOUR OR FIVE MAJOR DUTIES AND/OR ACCOMPLISHMENTS:

(Use bullets in front of each statement.)

1. _____

   _____

   _____

2. _____

   _____

   _____

3. _____

   _____

   _____

4. _____

   _____

   _____

5. _____

   _____

   _____

Professional Experience—Functional

Professional Experience:

Skill Heading _____

LIST FOUR OR FIVE MAJOR DUTIES AND/OR ACCOMPLISHMENTS:

(Use bullets in front of each statement.)

1. _____
   _____
   _____

2. _____
   _____
   _____

3. _____
   _____
   _____

4. _____
   _____
   _____
   _____

5. _____
   _____
   _____
   _____

CHAPTER 8   **W O R K S H E E T**

Professional Experience— Functional

Professional Experience:

JOB TITLE: _____

NAME OF EMPLOYER: _____

EMPLOYER'S CITY AND STATE: _____

DATES OF EMPLOYMENT (Month, Year):

From: _____ , 20_____ to _____ , 20_____

_____

JOB TITLE: _____

NAME OF EMPLOYER: _____

EMPLOYER'S CITY AND STATE: _____

DATES OF EMPLOYMENT (Month, Year):

From: _____ , 20_____ to _____ , 20_____

_____

JOB TITLE: _____

NAME OF EMPLOYER: _____

EMPLOYER'S CITY AND STATE: _____

DATES OF EMPLOYMENT (Month, Year):

From: _____ , 20_____ to _____ , 20_____

_____

JOB TITLE: _____

NAME OF EMPLOYER: _____

EMPLOYER'S CITY AND STATE: _____

DATES OF EMPLOYMENT (Month, Year):

From: _____ , 20_____ to _____ , 20_____

CHAPTER 9

EDUCATION

> **Highest level of education achieved (highest degree), graduation date, university or college attended, city, state**
>
> - Add special recognitions, achievements (high Grade Point Average, GPA), scholarships, awards, and any other highlights of your education (majors, minors, special courses), if the information is relevant to your career objective.
>
> - Mention professional training, workshops, seminars, and other informal education relevant to your objective here, too.
>
> - Position this section immediately after Objective or Summary of Qualifications if you are a recent graduate. Place extra emphasis on your education, detailing projects and achievements relevant to your career objective, since your Professional Experience will be limited.
>
> - Conversely, if you have worked for three or more years, highlight your present accomplishments, and reduce the emphasis on education. In this situation, you would position Education after Professional Experience.

YOUR EDUCATION IS RELEVANT!

Your education is important to your employer for two reasons. First, education equals skills. Employers will translate your education into skills you have acquired. They want people with skills that can help them. Indicate any areas of study, professional workshops, or special projects that display a skill area beneficial to an employer. Second, a university setting is similar to the workplace. A successful student, one with a high GPA or one who excelled in other areas, has ambition and drive—traits essential to succeeding in business. A successful student will be a successful employee.

Remember this and add any educational highlights that reflect your skill and expertise, as well as all accomplishments that demonstrate your ability to succeed. If you have other professional training, such as workshops or seminars, list them.

Even if you lack an outstanding educational history, do not omit this section. Obtaining a college degree is an accomplishment that most employers want. If you do not have a college background, indicate that you did graduate high school. Many jobs do not require more than a high school education, and the employer will want to be sure that you have at least earned your high school diploma.

If you mention your college degree, mentioning your high school diploma is unnecessary. However, list every college degree—B.A., M.A., and so forth. Begin with your last degree (or the degree you are presently working on). Use a reverse chronology and mention your other degrees or training.

If you supported yourself during college, you may add that fact. You might even state: "Earned 35 percent of my college expense" (or whatever percentage). This displays qualities that employers seek in an employee—initiative and drive.

EXAMPLE: **EDUCATION—RECENT GRADUATE**

EDUCATION: **M.B.A. Business Administration, 2006**
University of Florida—Miami Beach, FL
- Major: Financial Management
- Emphasis on Financial Forecasting
- Dean's List 2004–2006
- GPA 3.25/4.00
- Tuition paid via part-time employment as Financial Advisor

B.A. Economics, 2003
University of Illinois—Chicago, IL

EXAMPLE: **EDUCATION—EMPLOYEE WHO GRADUATED SOME YEARS AGO**

EDUCATION: **M.B.A. Business Administration, 2003**
University of Florida—Miami Beach, FL
Major: Financial Management

B.A. Economics, 2001
University of Illinois—Chicago, IL

Participated in weeklong seminar (Fall 2000):
"Financial Forecasting" with Martin Shanks.
Mastered more accurate methods for forecasting.

Notice the difference in these examples. The recent graduate details areas of expertise (emphasis on Financial Forecasting). Additionally, the recent graduate mentions such success indicators as Dean's List and 3.25 Grade Point Average on a scale of 4.00. (Some universities use a 5.00 grade scale, so including the scale is good, as in the above example.) Furthermore, the fact that the student tuition paid through work as a financial advisor is included. Employers will be impressed with this initiative and even more so with the use of college skills while gaining field experience.

The employee who graduated some years ago should not overemphasize education. Even mentioning a major is unnecessary, although it strengthens the resume if the objective is a job in finance. Mentioning the seminar is important because the employee gained a valuable skill (more accurate forecasting methods) that will benefit the employer.

ALWAYS TELL EMPLOYERS WHAT THEY WANT TO HEAR: THAT YOUR EDUCATION HAS EQUIPPED YOU WITH SKILLS AND QUALIFICATIONS THAT WILL BENEFIT THEIR ORGANIZATION.

WORKSHEET INSTRUCTIONS

Fill out the following practice worksheet.

If you are a college graduate, fill out the first section. You do not need to mention your high school if you have received a college degree or are working toward one.

Fill out all the information about your college—even if you are not a recent graduate. Later you will select the information to include in your resume.

You can abbreviate your degree (M.A., B.A., M.B.A., and so forth).

You can abbreviate your Grade Point Average (GPA).

Be sure to list the city and state of your college, university, or high school.

If you are currently seeking a college degree, the degree you are presently working on should come first. You can document it like this:

M.A. Program—Business Administration

UCLA, Los Angeles, CA

Additionally, if you have not yet received your degree, do not mention dates. If the employer wants to know, you can explain during the interview.

If you lack a college degree, complete the section on high school. If you have recently graduated high school (in the last year), you should also complete the section highlighting your high school experience. If you have been working for more than one year, do not include your high school accomplishments. Mentioning your high school and graduation date is sufficient.

If you have trade school or apprenticeship experience, complete the last section on special training. Furthermore, add any workshops, seminars, or special skills you have acquired (such as computer skills) that support your job objective and would benefit the employer.

If your "Special Training" skills are crucial to your job and deserve emphasis, you can devote an entire section heading to them.

Following the section on Education, you may add a new category: Special Training. Below this head list all special skills, such as computer expertise or other proficiency, that you have acquired through training.

CHAPTER 9 / WORKSHEET

Education Practice

IF YOU HAVE A COLLEGE EDUCATION

WHAT IS THE HIGHEST DEGREE YOU RECEIVED OR ARE PRESENTLY WORKING ON? _____

WHAT YEAR DID YOU GRADUATE? _____

WHAT COLLEGE OR UNIVERSITY IS YOUR DEGREE FROM?

Name: _____

City: _____ State: _____

YOUR MAJOR (if relevant to your objective): _____

YOUR MINOR (if relevant to your objective): _____

WHAT SPECIAL COURSES OR PROJECTS WOULD INTEREST YOUR EMPLOYER?

1. _____

2. _____

3. _____

WHAT SPECIAL HONORS, ACHIEVEMENTS, OR SCHOLARSHIPS DID YOU RECEIVE?

1. _____

2. _____

3. _____

4. _____

THESIS OR PUBLICATIONS:

1. _____

2. _____

WHAT OTHER DEGREES HAVE YOU RECEIVED? _____

FROM WHICH COLLEGE DID YOU RECEIVE THAT DEGREE?

Name: _____

City: _____ State: _____

YOUR MAJOR (if relevant to your objective): _____

CHAPTER 9 / WORKSHEET

Education Practice

IF YOU *DO NOT* HAVE A COLLEGE EDUCATION

DO YOU HAVE A HIGH SCHOOL DIPLOMA? WHICH HIGH SCHOOL?

Name: _____

City: _____ State: _____

Graduation Date: _____

IF YOU ARE A *RECENT* HIGH SCHOOL GRADUATE

LIST ANY AWARDS OR ACHIEVEMENTS YOU RECEIVED IN HIGH SCHOOL:

1. _____
2. _____
3. _____
4. _____

SPECIAL TRAINING

Trade Schools, Apprenticeships, Seminars, Workshops, etc.

LIST ANY INFORMAL EDUCATION THAT WOULD INTEREST YOUR EMPLOYER:

1. _____
2. _____
3. _____
4. _____

W O R K S H E E T   I N S T R U C T I O N S

Follow the guidelines below to select the most impressive information from your practice worksheet. Complete the education section on the following worksheet page exactly as you want it to appear on your resume.

Study the examples within the chapter and notice the format. The degree is bolded and important accomplishments are bulleted (●). You could use underlining, all caps, or even italics instead of boldface. The choice is yours. Make a note to the typist how you want your degree formatted. If you want your accomplishments emphasized with bullets, indicate bullet signs where you want them.

SELECTING THE MOST IMPRESSIVE INFORMATION

If you are a college graduate:

1. Begin with your most recent degree. Include your area of study: Do not write B.A., rather B.A. Psychology. On the same line, put your year of graduation.

   Two Exceptions:

   i. If you graduated long ago, omit the date.

   ii. If you took time off after college before working and the employer will notice a gap in your work history, omit the date. If the employer is interested, you can explain to him or her during the interview.

On the next line, write the name of the university or college, and on the same line, follow with the school's location—city and state.

Follow this with major areas of study, if relevant to your career objective:

B.A. Psychology, 1996

University of Southern California—Los Angeles, CA

Emphasis on Counseling and Abnormal Psychology

If you are a recent graduate:

1. List any important achievements, student activities, honors, and so forth that are relevant to your objective or demonstrate your ability to succeed. Emphasize this information with bullets.

If you have been in the workplace for more than two years:

1. Mention only those scholastic areas that will translate into skills for your employer. Accomplishments, GPA, and scholarships lose their importance the longer you have been out of school.

2. List any other *major* degrees, such as an undergraduate degree. Do not mention junior college if you have graduated from a university or college. Follow the same procedure in listing your other degrees, except decrease the emphasis on these less recent accomplishments and areas of study.

3. List any special graduate or informal training that you have received in workshops, seminars, or night school. Skip a line after your degree and university before listing any special training. Otherwise, it will appear as though you received this training at the university.

If you are not a college graduate:

1. Mention your high school and follow it with your year of graduation. Follow the exception above for when to omit your graduation date. On the next line, follow with the city and state of your high school.

   Rogers High School, 2002

   Chicago, IL

2. If you are a *recent graduate* follow the above rule for recent college graduates, listing relevant accomplishments, areas of study, and student activities.

3. Skip a line and list any special skills that you have acquired since high school, and where you acquired them (workshop or apprenticeship).

CHAPTER 9

WORKSHEET

Education

Education:

_____

_____

_____

_____

_____

_____

_____

_____

_____

_____

_____

Resume Style Guidelines:

College degree(s) should be: ☐ CAPS   ☐ **Bold**   ☐ *Italics*   ☐ Underlined

Other Instructions:
    Highlight all accomplishments with a: ☐ •   ☐ ✔   ☐ Other: _____
    The following mark indicates where the bullets should go: _____

ADDITIONAL QUALIFICATIONS

The end of your resume is a good place to highlight additional impressive qualifications and credentials that you could not fit elsewhere into your resume

Additional qualifications include:

- honors and awards
- publications
- membership in professional organizations
- licenses and accreditations
- foreign languages
- computer skills
- Web design
- digital photography
- special skills
- civic involvement
- military record
- hobbies, if relevant to your objective

VITAL INFORMATION THAT BELONGS IN YOUR RESUME

You can use a single catchall heading such as Additional Qualifications. Underneath, you can list all awards, honors, professional affiliations, and licenses. See Example 1.

If you would rather emphasize each of these, use a separate heading for each. For example, you could use a heading such as Licenses, and under it list the various licenses you have. Below that you could add another heading such as Professional Affiliations, and list under it all of your pertinent affiliations. See Example 2.

Choosing only qualifications that correspond to your career objective or demonstrate your ability to succeed is important. If you are applying for a job as a banker, do not mention your membership in a Ham Radio Club. However, that membership would interest an employer if you are seeking a job in radio and communications.

If you have multiple awards or memberships, you should use bullets to draw attention to them. See Example 1.

EXAMPLE 1:

ADDITIONAL QUALIFICATIONS:	• Fluent in French and Spanish • Member of International Law Associates • Frequent contributor to *Law Week*

EXAMPLE 2:

LICENSES:	1st Class FCC License
PROFESSIONAL:	Ham Radio Operators of North America
AFFILIATIONS:	Vice President (since 1993) R.B.A. (Radio Broadcasters of America)

W O R K S H E E T   I N S T R U C T I O N S

Decide how you want your additional information presented. If you want to emphasize multiple areas, such as honors and special training, decide if you want everything under one heading, such as Additional Information, or under two headings, such as (1) Honors, and (2) Special Training.

If your additional information consists of only honors, then use that as your heading.

Do not overdo it. Do not use more than two additional headings. Otherwise, you detract emphasis from the rest of your resume.

Complete the following worksheet page exactly as you want your additional qualifications to appear on your resume.

Look at the list of headings from the beginning of the chapter. Choose your heading or headings.

1. Write the heading(s).
2. List qualifications that are pertinent to that heading. If you have more than two qualifications under one heading, you should use bullets to emphasize and distinguish them.

WORKSHEET

Additional Qualifications

Heading #1: _____

QUALIFICATIONS: _____

_____

_____

_____

_____

_____

_____

_____

Heading #2: _____

QUALIFICATIONS: _____

_____

_____

_____

_____

_____

_____

_____

REFERENCES

REFERENCES AVAILABLE ON REQUEST—NO LONGER NECESSARY

Formerly, adding "References—Available on Request" at the end of the resume was customary. Today, it is unnecessary. Employers expect every applicant to have solid references. If you believe that you have exceptional references and want to direct the employer's attention to them, you may increase interest by writing "Excellent References Available on Request." The additional word "excellent" may raise the employer's interest. However, be sure you can deliver those outstanding references.

Never list your references on your resume. Save your list for the interview! If your references are famous, prestigious people, this is an exception where you may want to mention them in your resume.

Regardless, the employer will want references before he or she hires you, and he or she will probably ask you for them during the interview. Therefore, prepare a list of two or three references to take with you to the interview. In today's market, you can almost be certain a potential employer will check and double-check your references. Be sure the people you have chosen will give you an outstanding recommendation. If you are uncertain, do not list them.

Never assume your reference will automatically give you a good recommendation, as many may not remember your accomplishments the same way you do. Therefore, call your references on the phone first. Ask them if they will give you a good recommendation and if you can use them as references. Remind them of your past accomplishments, and update them on your present status. Moreover, send each a copy of your resume so that he or she has it nearby if an employer calls. Do not rely on a reference's memory. If an employer asks him or her about your accomplishments and he or she cannot remember, you will look bad and it will jeopardize your chances of being hired.

Your list of references should resemble your resume. It should have your contact information on your letterhead. The term "references" should follow in bold letters, all caps, and be centered. Underneath, list your references. Be sure to give full names, job titles, company names, companies' complete addresses, and phone numbers. Make it easy for the employer to contact your references. Study the example on the next page to see how to format your reference list. A sample format sheet follows on page 99.

1. Call your references and make sure they will give you good recommendations.

2. Send each a copy of your resume to review. It will remind and update them on your qualifications.

Posting Your References on Your Web Page

A new method of handling references is to include them on your Web page, assuming you maintain a Web page resume. You can link your references to the "References available" heading of your Web resume. You can also password protect this page, if you want it seen only by preferred persons. However, if you place the "References" page on your Web site, follow all the previous instructions and include all the relevant information, in case an employer wants to contact any of your references. Again, be sure that your references do not mind being a part of your Web site.

EXAMPLE:

REFERENCES

Melissa Brody
Sr. Vice President, Sales
Micro-Technics Computers
6787 North State Street
Des Moines, IA 90000
(555) 989-0098

W O R K S H E E T   I N S T R U C T I O N S

On the worksheet page, list your references *exactly* as you want them to appear on your final reference list.

On each succeeding line enter

- ↱ your reference's full name (if the gender is questionable add Mr. or Ms.).
- ↱ his or her position (job title).
- ↱ his or her company (full name).
- ↱ the company's address (include the suite number).
- ↱ the city, state, and zip code.
- ↱ your reference's area code/phone number/extension.

Make it easy for your potential employer to reach your references. Be sure to have at least one reference. If possible, have three.

RESUME STYLE GUIDELINES

Emphasize your references' names with boldface letters. You may even want to bold both their names and positions. This is especially appropriate if your reference person is well known or holds a powerful and highly respected position.

You may also consider centering your references and setting each off with a bullet (•) between them. (See the sample resumes in Chapter 12.)

Look at the example on page 97. Use the same paper stock (color and quality) as your resume.

Do not enclose your reference sheet with your resume—bring it with you to the interview.

Again, be sure your letterhead (contact information) appears on your Reference List. Thus, if your Reference List becomes separated from your resume, your employer will still know whose contacts these are.

EXAMPLE: SAMPLE REFERENCE SHEET

ANDRE WALKER   *1212 Sutton Drive*
                                                 Mountain Top, NY 90000
                                                      (555) 882-8789

REFERENCES

•

Tim O'Conner
Vice President Computer Operations
MacGraphics International
1334 Old Ridge Road
Wilton, OH 90000
(555) 897-0098

•

Ms. Yun-Ming Lee
Executive Vice President
Sealico Steel & Metal
700 Sparrow Lane
Tiger Creek, AK 90000
(555) 877-8768

•

Yolanda Haskins
Creative Director
Mountain Top Advertising
987 Winchester Plaza
Suite 865
Mountain Top, NY 90000
(555) 897-8700

WORKSHEET

References

1. _____
(name)

_____
(job title)

_____
(company)

_____
(address—street/suite number)

_____
(city, state, zip)

_____
(area code/phone number)

2. _____
(name)

_____
(job title)

_____
(company)

_____
(address—street/suite number)

_____
(city, state, zip)

_____
(area code/phone number)

3. _____
(name)

_____
(job title)

_____
(company)

_____
(address—street/suite number)

_____
(city, state, zip)

_____
(area code/phone number)

PUTTING IT ALL TOGETHER

THE SEQUENCE OF YOUR RESUME HEADINGS

If you have completed all the worksheets, you are now ready to put your resume together. Be sure you have finished your Summary of Qualifications, which should have been completed last.

Detach all of the worksheet pages, and place them in the proper sequence.

Your Contact Information is your letterhead and should come first.

Next is your Objective. If you believe the inclusion of an objective will limit your probabilities of getting many different types of jobs, you may omit it. However, as pointed out previously, most experts highly recommend including an objective or career goal. The objective will enhance your prospects of getting the job you want. Furthermore, with the increasing practice of information filing, you often need an objective to identify yourself for the proper job. If personnel is unsure what job you are applying for, your resume will be trashed rather than filed. If you want to apply for a broader job area, tell your employer about the other types of work you are willing to do in your cover letter.

Your Summary of Qualifications belongs next. This is optional. Use it if you have unique or outstanding qualifications that you want your employer to see immediately.

If you are a recent graduate, your Education section comes next, followed by your Professional Experience if you have any.

If you are not a recent graduate, your Professional Experience (chronological or functional format) comes next. In a functional-hybrid format you follow your Professional Experience with a short employment summary under the heading: Employment History. This is then followed by your Education.

End with any pertinent information such as Awards and Professional Affiliations.

If you have space remaining on the page, you can end with the proverbial "References Available on Request," although this is not required.

FORMATTING YOUR RESUME

If you do not have a word processing program with a laser printer, take your resume to a printing service. Most copy/print shops will do the job for under $25.00. This is money well spent. Remember, you want to project a professional image to ensure that your resume will get noticed. No one will read a messy resume, with clusters of words and long paragraphs staring at them. You need an eye-catching layout. This means short sentences with substantial white space. This means using bullets, caps, underlining, italics, and boldface to emphasize important information.

Check the sample resumes that follow to get an idea of an easy-to-read, inviting layout.

Print at least 50 copies of your resume on a good stock of paper such as one with linen or laid finish. The best color for a resume is off-white, eggshell, or gray. Ask the printer for samples of resume paper and choose one with an executive look.

Before you print your resume, complete the checklist that follows. After you have put your resume together, use this checklist to rate your resume. If your resume founders, fix it now before you spend money on printing it.

Furthermore, have someone who does not know you well read your resume. What image does it project to a stranger? Is it accurate? Have you included all the necessary information neatly, concisely, and correctly? If so, you have a solid resume. Additionally, have a friend proofread your resume.

Sometimes another person will notice flaws that you overlooked.

Resume Checklist

- ☐ My Contact Information is complete and correct.
- ☐ My e-mail address is included.
- ☐ My Objective is clearly defined.
- ☐ My resume is concise (no longer than two typed pages).
- ☐ My irrelevant personal information is excluded.
- ☐ My responsibilities and accomplishments are described by action verbs.
- ☐ My benefits to an employer are emphasized throughout.
- ☐ My image is that of a problem solver.
- ☐ My major accomplishments have all been mentioned.
- ☐ My accomplishments are described with concrete examples (supported by numbers or percentages).
- ☐ My resume format corresponds with my career goal.
- ☐ My past employers and job tasks are clear.
- ☐ My layout is eye-catching, with margins, indents, and headings that make it easy to read.
- ☐ My information is highlighted and emphasized with bullets.
- ☐ My paper stock is good and off-white or gray.
- ☐ *My resume presents a positive image of me!*
- ☐ *My resume projects a professional image!*

TO WRITE AND FORMAT ELECTRONIC RESUMES (E-RESUMES), SEE CHAPTER 16.

EXAMPLE: SKILLED WORKER WITH NO FORMAL EDUCATION—CHRONOLOGICAL FORMAT

MICHAEL THOMPSON

7988 North Brooks Road
Chicago, IL 90000
(555) 544-0987

OBJECTIVE	DRIVER/TRANSPORTATION MANAGER—where my extensive experience as a professional driver of straight trucks, my ability to train and supervise a driving crew, and my knowledge of warehouse management will be utilized to more efficiently run a transportation operations company.
PROFESSIONAL QUALIFICATIONS	• Outstanding driving record • Thorough knowledge of the Chicago area • Excellent physical condition—able to load heavy freight and operate lift gate • Dependable, hardworking • Always maintains good rapport with customers
EXPERIENCE 1994 to Present	Chicago Metro Delivery Service, Inc., Chicago, IL **DRIVER** Freight transportation in Chicago and surrounding environs Supervised crew of five Completed all invoices and standard order forms
1990 to 1994	Sugarette Delivery, Chicago, IL **DRIVER** Transporting materials throughout Illinois Responsible for inventory control
1987 to 1990	Metro-plex, Inc., Willmette, IL **ASSEMBLER** Assembly line—automotive vehicles Repair work
LICENSES & CERTIFICATES	• Class 2 License • D.O.T. License
REFERENCES	Excellent references available upon request

Example: Recent Graduate—Chronological Format

MARIA HERNANDEZ
Route 343
Nashville, TN 90000
(555) 989-8765
mhernand@juno.com

CAREER OBJECTIVE

Psychological Counselor for group or individual counseling in a hospital or rehabilitation center where my counseling experience combined with my sensitivity toward patients will result in superior handling of patients' needs.

EDUCATION

B.A. Psychology, 1999—University of Missouri, St. Louis, MO
- Emphasis on:
  - Clinical Problems in Childhood
  - Adolescent Psychology
  - Abnormal Psychology
  - Industrial and Organizational Psychology
- GPA 3.5/4.0 in major
- Dean's List—all four years
- Tuition paid via part-time employment, including working as a Psychological Counselor

PROFESSIONAL EXPERIENCE

Jan. 1999
to Present

VICTIMS SERVICE COUNCIL, Clayton, MO

Phone Counselor
- Provided victims of crime with moral support via outreach phone calls
- Assisted victims with food, medical, and counseling referrals

June 1997
to
June 1998

CAMP WYATT, Springfield, IL
Camp for Underprivileged/ Emotionally Disturbed Youths

Unit Director (Summer '98)
- Promoted from Counselor to Unit Director
- Trained and evaluated 15 counselors
- Designed and conducted workshops for counselors on camp procedures

Counselor (Summer '97)
- Worked with six- and seven-year-olds who required special attention in building social skills/ self-esteem
- Worked with senior citizens

FOREIGN LANGUAGES

Fluent in Spanish—reading and writing

EXAMPLE: E-RESUME FOR MARIA HERNANDEZ *(SEE CHAPTER 16 FOR MORE DETAILS.)*

MARIA HERNANDEZ
Route 343
Nashville, TN 90000
Phone: 555-989-8765
mhernand@juno.com

KEYWORD SUMMARY
Psychological counselor, group counseling, individual counseling, phone counselor, hospital, rehabilitation center, adolescent psychology, abnormal psychology, industrial psychology, organizational psychology, senior citizens, youths, crime victims, emotionally disturbed, crisis center, Bachelor of Arts, Psychology, dean's list, Spanish, sensitive, empathetic

CAREER OBJECTIVE
Psychological Counselor for group or individual counseling in a hospital or rehabilitation center where my counseling experience combined with my sensitivity toward patients will result in superior handling of patients' needs

EDUCATION
B.A. Psychology, 1999—University of Missouri, St. Louis, MO
• Emphasis on:
   − Clinical Problems in Childhood
   − Adolescent Psychology
   − Abnormal Psychology
   − Industrial and Organizational Psychology
• GPA 3.5/4.0 in major
• Dean's List—all four years
• Tuition paid via part-time employment, including working as a Psychological Counselor

PROFESSIONAL EXPERIENCE
Jan. 1999–Present
PHONE COUNSELOR—Victims Service Council, Clayton, MO
• Provided victims of crime with moral support via outreach phone calls
• Assisted victims with food, medical, and counseling referrals

June 1997–1998
UNIT DIRECTOR & COUNSELOR—Camp Wyatt, Springfield, IL
Camp for Underprivileged/ Emotionally Disturbed Youths
• Unit Director (Summer '98)
   − Promoted from Counselor to Unit Director
   − Trained and evaluated 15 counselors
   − Designed and conducted workshops for counselors on camp procedures
• Counselor (Summer '97)
   − Worked with six- and seven-year-olds who required special attention in building social skills/ self-esteem
   − Worked with senior citizens

FOREIGN LANGUAGES
Fluent in Spanish—reading and writing

EXAMPLE: CHRONOLOGICAL FORMAT—FUNCTIONAL EMPLOYMENT HISTORY

KISHA DANIELS
9898 West 54th St.
Rockford, IL 90000
Home: 555/990-0988 • Work: 555/997-0900 • kdaniels@aol.com

CAREER OBJECTIVE
Metallurgical Engineer in the capacity of **Production Supervisor**—where my extensive knowledge of alloys, my trouble-shooting ability, and my top managerial skills will increase productivity and lower costs.

SUMMARY OF QUALIFICATIONS
- Investigated and solved "stain" problem that Coral, Inc. (company's largest account) experienced with an alloy. My cost-efficient solution kept Coral a satisfied customer.
- Identified and solved serious "clogging" problem on a Wertli Casting machine, ultimately improving the output of the machine.
- Designed new technique of thin strip casting that reduced waste and cut production costs by more than 25 percent.

EMPLOYMENT HISTORY
Metallurgical Engineer / Production Supervisor   1991–Present
COBB INDUSTRIES, Rockford, IL

RESEARCH AND DEVELOPMENT
- Assisted Mineral Research Group in testing new materials
- Conducted experiments to establish new products

MANAGEMENT
- Supervised and guided staff of five engineers
- Prepared project costs and time estimates
- Determined equipment and raw materials modifications by maintaining close contact with representatives of equipment suppliers, *reducing operating costs by 12 percent*

PRODUCTION / TROUBLE-SHOOTING
- Designed and implemented cost-saving D.C. casting technique—still in use today
- Solved major stain problem for preferred customer, Coral
- Identified and solved serious mineral clogging problem on Wertli Casting machine

EDUCATION
Masters of Science—Metallurgy, 1990
University of Michigan, Detroit, MI

Associate Degree—Mining Technology
Haileybury School of Mines, Ontario, Canada
Areas of Study: Surveying and Extractive Metallurgy

SEMINARS & WORKSHOPS
- *Management by Objectives*—two-week workshop by Jake Peters, Ph.D., 1994
- *Finance for Nonfinancial Managers*—two-day course, 1996

EXAMPLE: FUNCTIONAL/HYBRID FORMAT

DAVID KATIDORIAN

1212 OTTER DRIVE
LOS ANGELES, CA 90000
(555) 889-8789
dkatidor@hotmail.com

PROFESSIONAL OBJECTIVE

SECURITY SYSTEMS TECHNICIAN—where my nine years of experience in installing and maintaining alarm and security systems, my expertise and knowledge of diverse control panels and their programming, and my proven ability to repair faulty systems will be utilized to improve productivity and increase efficiency and profits.

PROFESSIONAL EXPERIENCE

INSTALLATION/SUPERVISION

- Commercial and residential security systems
- Burglar and fire alarm systems—with patrol response
- Analyzed layout for proper placement of security sensors and equipment, eliminating future problems and complaints
- High-quality installations
- Contracted to supervise and check quality control of subcontracted installers and servicers

MAINTENANCE

- Repairing faulty systems
- Locating swinging circuits
- Locating ground circuits

PRODUCT DEMONSTRATION

- Conducted seminars for installers and servicers
  - Demonstrated security equipment and procedures
- Excellent customer communications skills
  - Ability to clearly instruct customers on system's use, thereby reducing future call-ins for assistance

EMPLOYMENT HISTORY

1993–Present   **INSTALLER/TECHNICIAN** (subcontractor)
Studio Security, Burbank, CA

1987–1993   **INSTALLER**
Bel-Air Patrol, Los Angeles, CA
(These L.A. firms service many demanding celebrities)

EDUCATION

Associate of Science Degree, School of Engineering
CAL-CEDA, Reseda, CA

CHAPTER 13

THE COVER LETTER

PURPOSE OF THE COVER LETTER

Many people think that the cover letter is just a formality and, at best, merely a device to draw the employer's attention to their resume. Consequently, they are content to write a nominal cover letter that simply directs attention to the enclosed resume and asks that it be reviewed. These people are putting their confidence entirely in their resume—and they are making a critical mistake.

The purpose of the cover letter is to make a favorable impression on the employer and to get you an interview. Frequently it is the well-crafted cover letter that gets the applicant an interview, not the resume. In today's market, where employers are more suspect of a resume's validity and integrity, the cover letter is gaining increasing importance. Often, a cover letter can do more than a resume, and the combination of both—a well-crafted cover letter and a strong resume—can give you the edge and the interview.

Electronic Cover Letters (E-Cover Letters)

In today's Internet and e-mail world, electronic cover letters are becoming common and are often replacing the standard cover letter reviewed here. In Chapter 16 the rules of writing and formatting an e-cover letter are discussed at length. However, most experts agree that it is essential to arm yourself with a well-executed, detailed cover letter as well. Mastering the techniques of writing an effective cover letter (as outlined in this chapter) is still crucial.

Additionally, many employers will not read any unsolicited e-mail because of the high volume of spam. Contacting an employer beforehand to ask if you may send him or her an e-mail or e-resume is best. Informing him or her in advance will also increase the chances of having your resume read.

EIGHT THINGS A COVER LETTER CAN DO

State What and Why

State exactly *what you can do* for the employer, and *why he or she should hire you*. Your resume is a history of your past, but your cover letter allows you to make a statement about your future. It allows you to specify in exact terms what you plan to do for the employer if you are hired. This requires research on your part. You will have to understand what problems employers are looking to solve and/or how your skills will benefit them. The entire focus of your cover letter should be on the benefits you will bring to the employer.

Make a Personal Connection

The resume is an impersonal document, written for a large audience. The main advantage of the cover letter is that it is personal. Each cover letter should be written to a specific company and, most important, directly to the person in charge of hiring. Finding out that person's name and addressing your letter to him or her personally (even if it is just to the head of personnel), can put you ahead of the competition.

Highlight Your Skills and Accomplishments

The cover letter can highlight skills and accomplishments that directly apply to the job at hand. By writing to a specific company with particular needs, you can highlight your most appropriate skills and customize each letter to emphasize the information that would most interest the employer to whom you are sending your resume. Ensure that your resume substantiates the skills mentioned in your cover letter. The cover letter should present a glimpse of what you can and will do for the employer, and it should help the employer predict and visualize your success in the job. If an employer can predict your performance better, your chances of getting an interview are greater.

Enthusiasm and a Positive Attitude

Convey enthusiasm and a positive attitude about the company with whom you are seeking employment. You will have to do some homework here too. Show the employers that you know what their organization is doing and demonstrate true interest in working for them. Nothing makes a better impression on employers than someone who compliments them and their organization.

Expand on Your Career Objective

If the job you are applying for does not match the career objective of your resume (or if your resume has no objective), use your cover letter to state your career objective and to expand upon it. Detail your qualifications to handle a new objective, referring to your resume for support.

Offer Additional Information

If you are changing jobs or you have been out of the workforce for a lengthy period and are worried that an employer will detect this from your resume, use your cover letter to explain. You may want to explain why you are changing jobs or why there is a large gap in your employment history. Be forewarned: do not direct the employer's attention to an issue if you do not have a reason that the employer will find acceptable. You may bring a plant closing or other reason for a job search that does not reflect poor workmanship on your part to the employer's attention in the cover letter. Always use your better judgment and, if in doubt, leave it out.

Be careful not to mention anything negative in your cover letter, as it could hinder you. Focus only on positive aspects and on what you can do to benefit the employer.

Thank an Employer for the Interview

Despite not being a true "cover letter" that accompanies a resume, a follow-up cover letter after an interview can be equally important. Many people underestimate the importance of sending a thank-you letter to an employer after an interview. This gesture demonstrates true interest on your part, and it allows you to add any information that you may have forgotten during the interview. Sometimes a small gesture of business etiquette such as a simple thank-you letter can affect how the employer perceives you.

Request an Interview

Although by sending a resume and cover letter you are implying you want an interview, it is imperative that you state the obvious in your cover letter. Do not rely on the employer to take action; that is, never end a letter with "If you are interested," "Please call me," or any other phrase that expects the employer to take action. *You* want the job, *you* take the action. Tell the employer you will contact him or her in the near future to arrange an interview. Then do so and follow up.

SIX COMPONENTS OF AN EFFECTIVE COVER LETTER

Your Contact Information

Use a letterhead with your name, address, phone number, and e-mail address. Matching the letterhead used in your resume is best.

Inside Address and Salutation

The most important feature of the cover letter is the fact that it is *personalized* and sent directly to the person in charge of hiring. If you are uncertain who this is, call the company. Furthermore, check and double check the spelling of the name. No one likes to see his or her name misspelled, and it shows carelessness on the writer's part. Get the person's title, too. The name and title will be followed by the company name and address.

Introduction: Expanding on Your Career Objective

In your introduction, state the purpose of your letter: identify the job you are seeking. Additionally, try to grab the reader's attention in the introduction. You can do this by highlighting an impressive accomplishment, mentioning the name of your referral, or by making an interesting observation or compliment about the company with whom you are seeking employment.

Include any additional information, such as reasons for making a job change or why this specific company interests you.

Highlight Your Background

Discuss your past. Highlight skills and accomplishments that are important for the job at hand. Refer to your resume (so that the employer will read it, too).

Tell the Employer What You Will Contribute to the Organization

Talk about your future. Explain how your background will benefit the employer. Interject your knowledge of the employer's accomplishments. Demonstrating that you did your homework can give you an edge over the competition.

Ask for an Interview

Take the initiative and tell the employer that you will call him or her to discuss further the matter on hand; that is, to arrange an interview.

Stick to this format as much as possible. Occasionally, you may want to switch the order of components four and five. Sometimes, first emphasizing the contributions you will make if hired and then reinforcing this with a summary of your background and experience is best. Either way, remember to always keep the employer in mind and always stress your ability and willingness to contribute to the organization.

THREE TYPES OF COVER LETTERS

Response to a Want Ad

When responding to a want ad, try to get the name of the person in charge of hiring and address your cover letter to him or her. If it is a blind ad, use a standard salutation of "Dear Sir/Madam," "Dear Friend," or even "Dear Boxholder."

The best format for answering a want ad is to match the requirements given in the ad with the skills you have listed in your resume. Show that your abilities correspond to the employer's needs. In many instances, this will replace components three and four.

Moreover, because a blind ad is impossible to follow up, you will have to end your letter cordially with a phrase such as: "Looking forward to your response." Then all you can do is wait!

Invited Response

Frequently, you will send your resume and cover letter to an employer you have spoken with on the phone; one who has requested you to send in the details of your work history and background. In this case, mention in your introduction: "Per our phone call . . ." or "As you requested. . . ."

In your letter you may also want to reference something you spoke about on the phone and expand upon it. Other than that, this type of cover letter will follow the standard format without deviation.

Referral's Lead

If a referral gives you a lead and you cannot reach this lead on the phone (or it is someone you would prefer writing to rather than speaking with on the phone), begin your introduction by mentioning the referral's name. Other than that, follow the preceding format.

SAMPLE COVER LETTERS

Letter #1: Response to a Want Ad

This cover letter focuses on matching the requirements of the ad with the applicant's skills. The ad appears in the shaded box in the right-hand corner of the letter.

Letter #2: Invited Cover Letter

This cover letter accompanies a resume that an employer has requested to see. This is usually after a phone conversation with a potential employer who has suggested that you send in your resume. Here the emphasis of the cover letter is on the benefits that you have to offer.

Letter #3: Referral's Lead

This is a cover letter sent on the suggestion of a referral, who is an acquaintance of the employer.

The letter's focus is on meeting the contact in person, either for an informational interview or to discuss a job opening.

Rules for Writing an Effective Cover Letter

1. Use a good stock of paper—use the same stock as your resume.

2. Use your letterhead—this projects a professional image, and if your letter is separated from your resume, the employer will have your contact information.

3. Keep your letter short—no longer than one page.

4. Date the letter.

5. Write to a specific person—preferably the one in charge of hiring.

6. Direct attention to your resume.

SAMPLE THANK-YOU LETTERS

Letter #1: After an Informational Interview

Sending thank-you letters to everyone who helps you in your job search, including friends or acquaintances that give you leads, is important. However, sending a thank-you letter to someone who has granted you an informational interview is crucial to your job search. (See Chapter 17, Networking.) This gesture can impress people enough that they work harder to find you more contacts or that they intervene on your behalf.

Letter #2: After a Job Interview

When an employer expresses interest and takes time to give you a job interview, it is imperative that you send a follow-up–thank-you letter. This common courtesy can sometimes be the factor that turns an employer's indecision in your favor. You would be surprised how many people remember a small consideration such as a thank-you letter. Sometimes, even after a rejection, if a thank-you letter is sent, the employer may consider the applicant for another job.

EXAMPLE: COVER LETTER #1

JUAN ORTEGA
1124 Bakery Avenue
Bakersville, NC 90000
(555) 998-0090

April 18, 2000

Teresa Micelli
Box 7344
Sunday Times
1123 N. Center Street
Bakersville, NC 11244

Dear Ms. Micelli,

I read with great interest your ad for Administrative Assistant, which appeared in the *Sunday Times*, July 14th. I am very enthusiastic because my background matches the qualifications you are seeking.

As you will note from my enclosed resume, I have more than five years experience in the field. I began as a secretary and worked my way up to an administrative position at Martel & Martel. I type 85 words per minute and am proficient in WordPerfect and Pagemaker.

I have always been complimented on the quality of my work and was personally responsible for designing our successful company newsletter.

Although I enjoy my current position, I would prefer a more challenging job where I can combine my creative talents and interpersonal skills.

I look forward to meeting with you in person to demonstrate that, along with my credentials, I have the personality that makes for a successful team player.

Sincerely,

Juan Ortega

EXAMPLE: COVER LETTER #2

SUSAN CHEN   1212 OTTER DRIVE
                                                      SMITHTON, NY 90000
                                                        (555) 889-8789

June 3, 2000

Michelle Irani
Process Engineer
Sealico Steel & Metal
700 Sparrow Lane
Tiger Creek, AK 90000

Dear Ms. Irani,

I enjoyed speaking with you on the phone earlier this week regarding a position with Sealico. Your division sounds exciting and your commitment to "total quality" is very impressive—a conviction I share with you.

As you can see from my enclosed resume, I have 12 years experience in metallurgy. At Pershall, my contributions as Process Engineer cut production costs by 14 percent and increased productivity.

I am optimistic that my knowledge and expertise in metallurgy, as well as my business experience in dealing with customers' needs and material selection, will be an asset to Sealico.

I look forward to meeting you personally and will follow-up this letter with a call next week to arrange a meeting at your convenience. I welcome the opportunity to prove that I can make an effective contribution to Sealico.

Sincerely,

Susan Chen

EXAMPLE: COVER LETTER #3

DASHEL JOHNSON
1212 SUTTON LANE
FARTHINGTON, PA 90000
(555) 979-8777

March 16, 2000

Anthony Tommasi
Vice President of Sales
Lesser & Lesser, Inc.
900 West Corvina Parkway
Marshalltown, IN 90000

Dear Mr. Tommasi,

Doris Chen, an associate of mine at Goodman Shoes, suggested that I contact you. As you may be aware, Goodman is presently experiencing a significant downsizing. I and three other sales managers will be discharged at the end of the month.

Doris tells me that you are always on the lookout for good salespeople. For the past ten years, I have managed the children's shoe department at Goodman, and under my management, our department was responsible for more than 40% of total shoe sales. I was also instrumental in developing a training program for new sales clerks that not only cut their "break-in" period but increased their efficiency as well. I have enclosed my resume for your review.

Mr. Tommasi, while I realize you may not have a position open for me now, I would very much like to meet with you at your convenience. I have a few ideas I feel could benefit Lesser & Lesser, which I am sure you will find useful. Additionally, I would greatly value any advice you can offer me concerning my job-hunting strategy.

I will call you next Thursday to see if we can arrange a convenient time to meet. Thank you for your assistance and I look forward to the opportunity of meeting with you personally.

Sincerely,

Dashel Johnson

EXAMPLE: THANK-YOU LETTER #1

DASHEL JOHNSON
1212 SUTTON LANE
FARTHINGTON, PA 90000
(555) 979-8777

April 3, 2000

Anthony Tommasi
Vice President of Sales
Lesser & Lesser, Inc.
900 West Corvina Parkway

Marshalltown, IN 90000

Dear Anthony,

I want to thank you for taking time from your busy schedule to meet with me last Tuesday. Your advice was quite helpful and as a result, I am reworking my resume to include many of your suggestions. I will send you a copy next week.

I very much appreciate the leads you gave me and have already set up a meeting with Milton Becker for next Friday. Please keep me in mind if you hear of any other openings.

I wish you continued success and hope I will have the opportunity of meeting you again.

Sincerely,

Dashel Johnson

EXAMPLE: THANK-YOU LETTER #2

SUSAN CHEN

1212 OTTER DRIVE
SMITHTON, NY 90000
(555) 889-8789

June 23, 2000

Michelle Irani
Process Engineer
Sealico Steel & Metal
700 Sparrow Lane
Tiger Creek, AK 90000

Dear Michelle,

I want to express my sincere appreciation for the interview on June 18th. The opportunity to meet you and become acquainted firsthand with the fine work you and your team have been doing, has strengthened my interest in working for Sealico.

I think your plan to implement a quality control checklist is excellent. I feel this is an area that I can be of great assistance to you. I am confident that my experience in setting up such a program will add to Sealico's efficiency and save you money.

Sealico is a dynamic and growing organization, and I would love to be part of your team. I hope I am extended the opportunity to prove that I can make an effective contribution.

Sincerely,

Susan Chen

THE JOB APPLICATION AND SKILL TESTS

THE RESUME IS NO LONGER ENOUGH

As the competition for jobs increases and the proliferation of resumes reaches an all-time high, more employers are seeking other means to obtain controlled and detailed information lacking in traditional resumes. Higher costs in conducting interviews and job training require employers to be increasingly cautious in screening candidates. Most employers are spending more time and money on extensive background checks for potential employees. Employers will easily uncover padded resumes and stretched truths about skills and background.

SKILL TESTS ARE BECOMING MORE CRUCIAL

A resume only reveals the information that the job seeker chooses to disclose. Conversely, applications may require the job seeker to offer information he or she may have omitted from a resume. Additionally, more employers are requesting various personality and skill tests to judge which candidates are better suited for a job. These detailed applications and skill tests are more comprehensive than a resume, allowing the employer to more accurately compare and evaluate candidates. Consequently, employers often rely *more* upon applications and skill tests than one's resume!

Although resumes and cover letters are still crucial job search documents, they are not single, decisive tools that employers use to screen applicants. Often, employers depend upon a system of "triangulation"—using three sources to supply information about a candidate. An employer will combine the resume, the application, and a battery of tests, ranging from simple skill tests to complex personality tests (psychometric testing), to verify a job applicant's qualifications. This triangle of documents must merge effectively to ensure that the job seeker obtains an interview. A resume is no longer enough, and today's job seeker must be ready for more.

BACKGROUND CHECKS

More employers today are becoming suspicious of significant inaccuracies found on candidates' resumes. Many larger firms are hiring professional background-checking companies. Background-screening companies have grown from just a handful five years ago to over 700 companies today. Some companies screen over one million resumes a year. Some claim that as many as 14 percent of applicants lie about their education. Many employers will fire an employee if they discover falsehoods in his or her resume. They are concerned that an employee who lies on a resume is likely to lie and cheat at work too.

Candidates should never stretch the truth on their resume or color it with a few "little white lies." The employer may do a professional background check, and any padding or fibs may cost you the interview and job.

SKILLS TESTING AND APTITUDE TESTS

The rising costs of employee training and the increased percentage of turnover are causing employers to utilize tests in helping them predict if a candidate fits the job.

Frequently, employers will administer personality and skill tests in order to ascertain if the candidate's resume and claims are true. Skill tests can include everything from a mechanical aptitude test (for many technical jobs) to tests that check vocabulary, grammar, and simple math skills. More complex examinations test problem-solving skills, such as those found in "case interviews." (See page 153.) Employers will not interview job seekers who score poorly. You cannot prepare for these tests, and the only advice is to remain calm and do your best work if confronted with this situation.

PERSONALITY TESTS

A test that assesses a candidate's ability to do the job based on his or her personality is trickier. Personality or *psychometric tests* try to determine interpersonal skills, honesty, and work ethic. All candidates take the same tests; thus, employers can easily compare scores and more accurately choose candidates. If someone were applying for a sales job, yet scored low on "social outgoing skills" or level of "persuasiveness," he or she would be a poor choice for the job.

These tests can also select or "screen in" a candidate, rather than screen one out. Sometimes, if a person has a low score for a particular job, but his or her score is considerably higher for another available job, he or she may get a more appropriate job. Additionally, people whose resumes are weak and normally would be discarded may be offered the job because they received high scores on their skill and personality tests.

Besides testing for sociability, these tests score factors such as assertiveness, flexibility, risk taking, thoroughness, time management, organizational qualities, teamwork, leadership skills, honesty, and integrity. Questions may have you choose words that most and least describe you. You may be asked to talk about things you enjoy doing or how you would react in specific situations.

Rising numbers of padded resumes, as well as the high cost of training and keeping employees, have made employers more suspicious about trusting resumes alone. While still a vital tool in your job search, be aware that your resume will be scrutinized. An employer may use a background check, a skill test, and even a psychometric test before giving you an interview. Tests have become sophisticated, and a candidate can rarely fool or second-guess these tests. Remember, nothing can be done to prepare for these tests and the only advice is to answer truthfully. Do not feel depressed about losing a job due to low scores on these tests. If you do not fit the job, it probably would not satisfy you and you are better off finding employment elsewhere.

THE JOB APPLICATION

The job application, in particular, has gained a integral role for two reasons. One, because applications are tailored directly for the job at hand, the questions are designed to supply the employer with the exact information he or she requires to properly screen applicants. Usually the employer wants to ascertain quickly that the applicants have the required skills, training, and experience to perform the job. Second, because each applicant is answering the same questions, employers can better compare applicants to see which are best qualified and thus warrant the time spent on interviewing and ultimately training.

ANSWER ACCURATELY AND HONESTLY

Completing these applications accurately and thoughtfully is imperative because they are an integral screening tool. If possible, complete an application at home where you can think about it. If you must complete it in the employer's office, ask for two applications so that if you make a mistake you can fix it. Bringing a small pocket dictionary to check your spelling is smart.

Be sure you reread each question and that you answer each completely. Often, only small spaces are allotted and you must be succinct—brief yet exact—in completing these forms. As in your resume, use action verbs that emphasize your accomplishments.

Never leave an answer blank, as the employer may mistakenly think that you have not carefully read the application or that you have chosen not to answer a specific question. If the question does not apply to you, mark it N/A (not applicable).

Answering all questions *honestly* is imperative, as more employers are checking applicants' backgrounds. A signed job application is a legal document, and many employers keep them on file. Falsifying information may not only disqualify a candidate, but often the employer will terminate one's employment if he or she later discovers dishonesty. Sometimes, an employee can be held liable for losses he or she has caused the employer due to giving dishonest information regarding his or her skill level and background.

OMIT NEGATIVE INFORMATION

If asked why you left your last job, never write "Fired." Do not write anything negative on your application. Simply write, "Job was terminated" or "Wanted to advance with more challenging career." Furthermore, never write disparaging remarks about a past employer or company. Employers do not want to hire people who slur others or who have a negative outlook. On an application, less is usually more.

EXPECT "INTERVIEW QUESTIONS" ON THE APPLICATION

Applications are becoming more and more comprehensive, with employers asking questions that were normally regulated to the interview. Finding an application that asks, "Why do you want to work for our company?" is common. Even such questions as, "How would you resolve a conflict with a coworker?" or "What are your long term goals?" are now on applications. Therefore, review "interview questions" and your answers before completing an application.

Many employers require applicants to complete their forms on a computer or even online. Even those written in pen may be scanned into a computer database. Like e-resumes, many of these applications will be electronically sorted and selected based upon keywords.

THE JOB APPLICATION MAY BE YOUR FIRST IMPRESSION

Your application may be the first document the employer reviews, so make a good first impression. Ensure that you have answered all questions and have included all critical information. Your application should be well written, with correct spelling and grammar, and most importantly, be neat. Sometimes simply a neat and well-written application will give you the edge. Additionally, bring a copy of your resume with you. Many employers will welcome an application with an attached resume and/or cover letter. A neat and well-written resume will attest to your professionalism and will strengthen your chances of receiving an interview.

PREPARE AN APPLICATION DATASHEET

The job application will require more detailed information than your resume (such as complete addresses and phone numbers of past employers, Social Security number, and so forth). Therefore, preparing an application datasheet to take with you when you apply for a job is crucial. When you are required to complete an application on the spot, you should not rely on your memory, which could fail you and force you to return another day to complete the application. Meanwhile, another applicant may be hired. Be prepared. Bring your application datasheet, resume, and pocket dictionary with you! Remember, you can never be too prepared.

FOLLOW UP APPLICATIONS WITH A PHONE CALL OR LETTER

Treat the application like a resume and follow up with a phone call (and/or cover letter) a few days after submitting the application. Demonstrate that you are interested in the position and request an interview. When you receive an interview, bring a copy of your resume and job application (if possible) for reference.

Job Application Checklist

- [ ] Bring a copy of your "Application Datasheet."
- [ ] Bring a copy of your resume (and cover letter).
- [ ] Bring a pocket dictionary.
- [ ] Use a black ballpoint pen.
- [ ] Print neatly—In case the application is scanned into a computer, printing rather than using cursive lettering is imperative.
- [ ] Read every question carefully.
- [ ] Answer every question concisely.
- [ ] Use action verbs to describe your accomplishments.
- [ ] Use as many "keywords" as possible.
- [ ] Include all vital information.
- [ ] Mark all questions that do not apply with N/A.
- [ ] Answer all questions honestly.
- [ ] Reread the application and correct any mistakes.
- [ ] Date and sign the application —Many employers will not accept unsigned applications.
- [ ] Attach a resume (and cover letter) when possible.
- [ ] Follow up with a phone call (or personalized cover letter) 1–3 days later to request an interview.

Application Data Sheet

Many of these questions may not be asked on the application, but as mentioned, it is better to prepare for all situations.

PERSONAL INFORMATION

NAME (AS IT APPEARS ON ALL LEGAL DOCUMENTS) _____

Be careful. Some applications ask for "Last Name First", some don't. Be sure to carefully read the application.

MAIDEN NAME _____

SOCIAL SECURITY NUMBER (SSN) _____

DRIVERS LISCENSE (STATE AND NUMBER) _____

BIRTHDATE _____

NUMBER OF DEPENDENTS _____

PERMANENT ADDRES _____

_____

_____

PAST ADDRESS _____

_____

HOME PHONE _____

CELL PHONE _____

ANSWERING MACHINE _____

In some instances a family member or relative or service may take your calls, be sure that number is readily available to the employer.

FAX NUMBER _____

EMAIL ADDRESS _____

PAST CONVICTIONS / CRIMINAL RECORD

Nature of the offense, date and location of conviction, and the sentence or probation may also be requested.

Some jobs cannot be held by persons with a criminal record. It is very important to be honest as this information is usually checked. For some jobs a certificate from the local police department (including fingerprinting) may be required.

(continued)

Application Data Sheet

JOB AT HAND

POSITION YOU ARE APPLYING FOR _____

Be specific and be realistic. Be sure the job you are applying for matches up with your skills and experience. You may also be asked to list a "second choice"

DATE YOU ARE AVAILABLE TO START _____

"Immediately" or "open" shows you are ready to start work now or at any future time. If you have to give your present employer notice, take that into consideration when answering.

HOURS YOU ARE AVAILABLE TO WORK _____

Morings, Evenings, or Open (if you can work any shift).

SALARY REQUIREMENTS _____

You can request "standard rate". However, in this case it is best to be noncommittal and write "negotiable" or "open," which means you will negotiate with the employer at the time you are offered the job.

EMPLOYMENT HISTORY

Unlike your resume which only requires the employers' city and state, most applications require each employer's complete address and usually phone number. Most applications want the name of your past supervisor as well as permission to speak to him about your performance. Past salary history and specific reasons for leaving past employment may also be requested.

CURRENT EMPLOYER _____

JOB TITLE _____

COMPLETE ADDRESS OF EMPLOYER _____

_____

EMPLOYER'S PHONE NUMBER _____

NAME OF SUPERVISOR _____

DUTIES _____

_____

_____

Try to use "action verbs" and "key words". Also be sure to stress your accomplishments and employer benefits you provided.

DATES OF EMPLOYMENT _____

SALARY _____ (per year or per hour)

REASON FOR LEAVING _____

Try to find a "positive reason"—sought more challenging position, desire to advance, etc. If you were fired simply write "position terminated." Try to eliminate any negative answers.

PAST EMPLOYER #2 _____

JOB TITLE _____

COMPLETE ADDRESS OF EMPLOYER _____

_____

EMPLOYER'S PHONE NUMBER _____

NAME OF SUPERVISOR _____

DUTIES _____

_____

_____

DATES OF EMPLOYMENT _____

SALARY _____ (per year or per hour)

REASON FOR LEAVING _____

PAST EMPLOYER # 3 _____

JOB TITLE _____

COMPLETE ADDRESS OF EMPLOYER _____

_____

EMPLOYER'S PHONE NUMBER _____

NAME OF SUPERVISOR _____

DUTIES _____

_____

_____

DATES OF EMPLOYMENT _____

SALARY _____ (per year or per hour)

REASON FOR LEAVING _____

SKILLS AND CERTIFICATIONS

JOB SKILLS _____

COMPUTER SKILLS (programs you are proficient at) _____

(continued)

Application Data Sheet

KEYBOARD SKILLS _____ (words per minute—wpm)

FOREIGN LANGUAGES _____

CERTIFICATIONS _____

EDUCATION

DEGREE EARNED _____

MAJOR _____

MINOR COURSES _____

UNIVERSITY / TECHNICAL SCHOOL _____

GRADE POINT AVERAGE (GPA) _____

CLASS RANK _____

ACCOMPLISHMENTS / HONORS _____

_____

STUDENT ACTIVITIES AND ORGANIZATIONS _____

_____

VOLUNTEER WORK _____

_____

PROFESSOR / ADVISOR _____

PHONE NUMBER _____

REFERENCES

NAME _____

ADDRESS _____

_____

PHONE NUMBER _____

EMAIL ADDRESS _____

RELATIONSHIP TO YOU _____

Such as former boss, professor, clergy, business acquaintance, and so on

YEARS YOU HAVE KNOWN REFERENCE _____

NAME 2 _____

ADDRESS _____

_____

PHONE NUMBER _____

EMAIL ADDRESS _____

RELATIONSHIP TO YOU _____

YEARS YOU HAVE KNOWN REFERENCE _____

NAME 3 _____

ADDRESS _____

_____

PHONE NUMBER _____

EMAIL ADDRESS _____

RELATIONSHIP TO YOU _____

YEARS YOU HAVE KNOWN REFERENCE _____

MISCELLANEOUS QUESTIONS

Many of these questions are similar to those asked during an interview. For more examples see pages 156–157.

Why do you want to work for our company?

What contribution do you feel you can make for our company?

What is the most common misconception about you?

What are your long term goals?

How would you attempt to resolve a dispute with a coworker?

FORMER MILITARY PERSONAL

Either in addition to past work history or in place of it, you will be asked questions regarding you military record. You may even be asked to bring your discharge papers.

ENTRY & DISCHARGE DATES _____

TYPE OF DISCHARGE _____

BRANCH _____

LAST RANK _____

SPECIAL TRAINING AND SKILLS _____

THE INTERNET AND YOUR JOB SEARCH

UTILIZING THE WEB IN YOUR JOB SEARCH

The Internet is the one facet of job search that has changed the most dramatically. Initially, everyone assumed that the Net would become the ideal job search resource. Job openings could easily be posted and resumes could effortlessly be sent forth. Unfortunately, this has not materialized to the degree predicted. The onslaught of resumes on the more popular job boards has produced as little as a 5 percent success rate. Furthermore, with so many employers posting job openings, the number of options can be overwhelming. Some larger boards have over 100,000 job listings! Too many resumes and too many choices have made this overcrowded and overworked area of job search somewhat ineffectual. Even local newspaper want ads have proven to be more effective than the so-called specialized Internet job boards.

PRIVACY ISSUES ON INTERNET JOB BOARDS

Moreover, new concerns regarding privacy issues have also surfaced. Author Pam Dixon, an expert on online job search, is now supervising a Web site (<http://worldprivacyforum.org>) to educate the public on job scams and frauds that have resulted from dishonest individuals accessing resume databases. Some of her tips on safely posting a resume on the Net will be discussed in detail later in this chapter, and checking her Web site before posting your resume on the Web is always a good idea.

E-MAIL IS CRUCIAL IN TODAY'S JOB SEARCH

E-mail has remained the one area of job search in which the Web continues to be indispensable. Having an e-mail address is crucial, as many employers may want to contact you via e-mail. Many services such as Yahoo! and Hotmail offer free e-mail accounts, and having one is necessary, as is including it on your resume in your contact information. Again, as mentioned in an earlier chapter, having a separate e-mail account dedicated to your job search is a good strategy. Additionally, be conservative in choosing an e-mail address name. Comical names such as "hicks-r-us" or "motorcycle_babe_24" could give a prospective employer qualms.

FOUR EFFECTIVE WAYS OF USING THE WEB IN YOUR JOB SEARCH

Although, it has not been as successful as predicted, one should not shun the Web completely. The Web can be utilized successfully, but remember that many of the rules have changed. You should maximize your use of the Web and concentrate on the most advantageous areas of the Internet. The most effective use of the Internet in today's job search falls into four main areas.

1. Accessing corporate-maintained Web sites, which post jobs available at that particular company only.

2. Accessing specialized job boards that cater to your specific career.

3. Researching online trade journals and industry-related articles to uncover job leads and names of people you can directly submit your resume to.

4. Networking—uncovering the names and identities of people who can assist you in your job search by joining newsgroups, forums, mailing lists, chat rooms, and blog groups.

Remember, whatever options you pursue on the Web, have a top-notch e-resume, replete with the most effective keywords, ready to upload electronically if necessary. With the onslaught of resumes posted on the Web, having one that stands out in the crowd is especially important.

CORPORATE WEB SITES

Posting resumes directly on a target company's dedicated Web site is more effective than posting on generic job boards. Previously, many corporations relied on the larger job boards to find candidates. However, this is now changing and for the better. Today, most large companies maintain their own Web sites. Here potential employees can learn more about the company and decide if the environment and work meets their career goals. One warning: Remember, what you read on a company's own Web site is controlled information—they are telling you *only* what they want you to know. To find a more unbiased view, you should investigate them further. Search for the company online and read newspaper and journal articles about them. If you log onto either PR Newswire <http://www.prnewswire.com> or Business Wire <http://www.businesswire.com>, you can search for a company's news, including recent press releases. You will discover what is happening at your target company, and you can learn what new developments are occurring in your industry.

LOOK FOR "BUZZWORDS" USED ON CORPORATE WEB SITES

Corporate Web sites can be helpful in other ways as well. Take note of the buzzwords the company site uses and incorporate those same keywords into your resume and cover letter. Be sure to read their Mission Statement. This will depict where they are headed, and it will inform you of the information you should include in your cover letter. If your cover letter can explain how you can help the company achieve its "mission," you will already have one foot in the door.

Of course, the most important reason to check a company's Web site is to uncover job leads in your specific field. Usually, a firm will post all jobs available in all departments. Unlike the larger job boards, the jobs posted on a corporate job board currently exist, and candidates who answer these ads will normally be considered quickly. If your skills and experience match the job description, posting a resume directly on a company Web site gives you a greater chance of getting an interview than posting on a larger, generic board does.

GATHER INFORMATION FOR YOUR INTERVIEW

Furthermore, if you are granted an interview, the research and information you glean from a company Web site can be enormously helpful in preparing you for the interview. You can learn about the job and about the company's future. Knowing the background and outlook of the company is advantageous in an interview.

HOW TO FIND A SPECIFIC CORPORATE WEB SITE

Finding a specific company or list of companies that would be interested in your skills is a simple process. A few of the most common methods for tracking down target employers' Web sites follow.

1. Search engine: Using your desired job title and/or keywords that describe your skills will produce many hits.

2. Yellow Pages: You can search through them either online or in print.

3. Trade journals: You can search through them either online or in print.

4. Want ads: You can find many newspapers online, and check the classifieds there.

Once you have found the name of a potential target company, you can use a search engine to find if they maintain a home page or dedicated Web site. Once you have located the Web site, navigating it usually involves clicking on options from a menu. This is perhaps the most effective way to uncover effective job leads.

Although accessing corporate Web sites is one way to exploit the Web, remember that nothing replaces face-to-face personal contact. Ultimately, most jobs are filled by people who contact their friends and acquaintances to steer them toward a job opening. Nonetheless, approach the Web as one option in your job search. Do not rely upon an exclusively Internet job search. Never let it replace more sophisticated "networking" to uncover leads.

SPECIALIZED JOB BOARDS AND TRADE JOURNALS

Many professional associations maintain job boards dedicated to a specific job area, such as health care (<http://www.healthcareerweb.com>). These, too, can usually be found via search engines and trade journals. Numerous trade journals now appear on the Web, some for free. A free health-career journal such as <http://www.healthindustrynews.com> can be an indispensable source for keeping up with the health profession, and can garner many names of people and potential employers to utilize in your job search. Many specialized and regional job boards abound on the Web. These provide a greater chance of getting your resume to the right person in the right place than the more popular, generic job boards.

NETWORKING ON THE WEB

Networking means building relationships with people. While face-to-face contact will always be the best method for this, the Net can help initiate long-term business relationships. Besides corporate Web sites and trade journals, you can uncover many valuable leads by networking on the Web via newsgroups, message boards (forums), chat rooms, mailing lists, and blogs. For privacy reasons, you should guard your identity as well as the amount of information you divulge until you are certain who you are contacting.

NEWSGROUPS, FORUMS, AND MAILING LISTS

A countless number of newsgroups exist on the Web devoted to employment and job search. Newsgroups are specialized bulletin boards for online discussion. Each newsgroup is devoted to a specific topic or area of interest, and visitors post and read messages. The groups are called "forums" and all the postings that regard one topic or question are called "a thread." These newsgroups are categorized either by specific industries, such as those that deal exclusively with jobs in computer programming, or by location, such as Chicago.

Many people strongly believe that the newsgroups and forums are actually the best source of job leads on the Net because they are more focused and personal. Newsgroups encourage you to post messages and interact with people in your profession. Many of the people you "meet" in a newsgroup can personally help you. Newsgroups give you exposure to prominent people in your field, and managers and personnel looking to hire sometimes frequent them. Furthermore, people in newsgroups are often sympathetic and helpful to fellow posters, making this a perfect arena for networking. Many are eager to give advice and even names of people who are hiring. They can also inform you on job-related topics such as benefits and pay scales, which may help you negotiate when you receive a bona fide offer.

Read the Frequently Asked Questions (FAQs) page if one exists. This will acquaint you with the subject matter discussed in the forum or chat room and will answer many questions you have regarding the group. Additionally, practice proper "netiquette." Bad language or obnoxious postings may get you removed from a group. Always remember that many prospective employers also surf these groups in hopes of finding recruits, so it pays to be particularly careful when you post. Furthermore, merely reading the posts will not help much. If you truly want to network, be active in these groups. Always be professional. When you make "contact" with someone you feel will be helpful, contact them directly via e-mail.

Mailing lists can also help you uncover leads. Mailing lists (listservs) are basically discussion groups carried on via e-mail. Postings do not appear on a board but are e-mailed to each member individually. When you answer or post a message, each member on the list receives your message in his or her e-mail. Mailing lists perform the same networking function as newsgroups but are smaller and more personalized. You must first subscribe to become a member, and unlike newsgroups, many of the lists are not open to everyone. Many mailing lists keep archives of their postings. To finds mailing lists and newsgroups visit <http://groups.yahoo.com>.

ADDITIONAL USES OF THE WEB IN YOUR JOB SEARCH

A final important and often overlooked, helpful area of the Web is its yellow and white pages. Use these to track down former classmates or friends who may help you in your job search. Networking has proven to be the most successful means of finding a job, and the Internet can prove extremely effective in this area.

Besides online methods for conducting a job search, do not forget the wealth of online information to help you in assessing your skills, as well as articles galore on effective job search protocol. Tips on everything from writing your resume and cover letter to job interview questions are online. The Web also can enlighten you about current trends and the constantly changing markets in your profession. Use the Web, but do not have unrealistic expectations about the outcome. Finding a job is hard work and the Web provides just one tool in your job search toolkit. However, if you integrate it with other more traditional job search methods, you will succeed.

PRIVACY ISSUES ON THE WEB

Before ending this chapter, you should be aware of privacy issues that have recently become a serious concern to online job searchers. When you post your resume on the Net, many people besides bona fide employers may have access to this private information. To protect yourself, post only on sites that offer "anonymous posting" where your true identity is masked until a legitimate employer enquires. Never give your Social Security or your driver's license numbers over the Net—even if a so-called employer contacts you and tells you that he or she needs it for a background check. Moreover, be wary of employment offers that involve working from home or transferring money— many of these are scams. For more information, visit Pam Dixon's Web site: <http://worldprivacyforum.org>. This Web site has many tips and articles on how to safely post your resume online. This Web site is frequently updated and offers the timeliest information regarding privacy issues and job scams.

CHAPTER 15 / WORKSHEET

Using the Internet in Your Job Search

LIST OF WEB SITES TO CHECK OUT

JOB POSTINGS

http://www.delmar.com _____

_____

_____

_____

MESSAGE BOARDS

_____

_____

_____

_____

NEWSGROUPS

_____

_____

_____

_____

MAILING LISTS

_____

_____

_____

_____

COMPANY WEB SITES

_____

_____

_____

_____

(continued)

Using the Internet in Your Job Search

TRADE JOURNALS ONLINE

_____

_____

_____

_____

CHAT ROOMS

_____

_____

_____

_____

SEARCH INDEXES/YELLOW-WHITE PAGES

_____

_____

_____

_____

OTHERS

_____

_____

_____

_____

NOTES:

ELECTRONIC RESUMES, PORTFOLIOS, AND OTHER NEW RESUME FORMATS

ELECTRONIC RESUMES: WHY YOU NEED ONE

Two dramatic changes in today's workplace have radically altered the art of resume writing: the prevalence of computers in everyday business and the ever-growing impact of the Internet. As computers became widespread, many companies turned to resume-tracking systems to scan incoming resumes and transfer the information into a database for easy retrieval. An electronic "search" that uses keywords and phrases to describe the perfect candidate can quickly select the most qualified applicants. Having a computer sort and select potential candidates is faster and cheaper. Resumes written and printed expressly for scanning are "scannable resumes." Those formatted specifically to be sent via e-mail or to be posted directly to a computer database are referred to as electronic resumes or e-resumes. The proliferation of computer technology in selecting candidates has further intensified the need to have a resume that is "computer friendly," one that can be read accurately and favorably by a computer.

Today, even the most beautifully printed resumes sent by mail to an employer may never be seen by the hiring personnel. Instead, a secretary may feed your "masterpiece" into a scanner, and an interested employer will view the unadorned electronic version, not the dolled-up one.

SEND EACH EMPLOYER *TWO* VERSIONS OF YOUR RESUME

In addition to sending a high-quality formatted copy of your resume to an employer (and you should, because not every employer uses sophisticated resume-tracking programs), *you must also send an e-resume version*. It should be identified (preferably with a Post-it note) as the "scannable version," and formatted to be scanned easily and accurately. It must be

↪ Formatted in ASCII. (ASCII is an acronym for American Standard Code for Information Interchange and is simply a text-only file that contains no special formatting codes.) This version of your resume must not contain boldface, italic, underlining, fancy fonts, bullets, or anything that a scanning program finds difficult to read. Consider the kind of document produced on old typewriters, before boldface and fancy fonts were prevalent.

↪ On clean, white paper (the brighter the better), standard size (8½ 11"), printed with a laser printer (or a top-of-the-line ink-jet printer) in black ink, and sent unfolded (in a large envelope). The creases in a fold can cause letters to crack or fade, which will confuse scanning software. A complete list of formatting rules for e-resumes is found later in this chapter.

E-resumes on the Internet are the same. While most e-mail programs allow you to "attach" a document, allowing you to send your beautifully formatted work into cyberspace, an employer may not have the same word processing or publishing program you used to create your document. If an employer does not have the corresponding program, he or she will be unable to open your file, and your resume will be lost. Although most businesses use Microsoft Word, it is not a standard and unless an employer specifically asks for an MS Word attachment, do not send one. This leaves the "plain vanilla" ASCII resumes that computers like best.

ADVANTAGES OF THE E-RESUME

E-resumes do offer advantages. First, they are cheaper. You do not need to spend money on fancy paper and printing fees. You will also save postage fees, because you will send most of your resumes via e-mail or post them directly to job boards. Furthermore, most employers who maintain resume databases will store your resume for longer. Even if you are not hired initially, your resume will stay active and you may be hired later.

HOW TO STAND OUT IN ASCII

However, one dilemma exists. On the one hand, competition today is fierce. With more people changing jobs and job databanks holding tens of thousands of resumes, standing out is critical. On the other hand, resumes have been reduced to bland, plain-text documents, where one aesthetically looks the same as another, which makes standing out nearly impossible.

The solution is the content of your resume—what you say about your skills and accomplishments—and how you present yourself. This, rather than the fancy formatting and paper, will distinguish you. In a recent phone interview, resume expert Peter Newfield stressed that today's resumes must be *more results driven than skills driven*. Your resume must stress employer benefits—how you saved your company money, how you increased revenue and profits, or even a list of your communication skills. Display the value that you will add to the company, and demonstrate what the company will gain by hiring you. This will distinguish your resume from the competition. (For more details on employer benefits, refer to Chapter 2.)

Nevertheless, even with a top-notch resume, you can still go unnoticed for one simple reason: the computer selects candidates based upon keywords in your resume. Even if your resume is outstanding, if it does not contain the exact keywords the computer is searching for, it will not be selected. Today, what you do not put in your resume, namely the proper keywords, is an impairment. Unfortunately, a person with a mediocre resume who included the proper keywords has a better chance of being chosen than a person who is more qualified but neglected using the proper keywords. To compete, you must understand how to carefully select keywords and integrate them successfully into your resume.

Although the object is to make your resume computer friendly, never forget that eventually a person, namely the person interested in hiring you, will read it. Never lose the "human touch." The task is to make your resume readable and convincing, yet computer friendly (that is, loaded with keywords).

KEYWORDS AND HOW TO CHOOSE THEM

The basic content of your e-resume should remain the same as your formatted one; it should highlight your experience, education, skills, responsibilities, achievements, and most importantly, the benefits you offer the employer. The only significant difference in the content will be the addition of keywords in your e-resume.

Some believe that keywords should appear under their own major heading, labeled Keywords or Career Highlights. Others suggest integrating them into the Summary of Qualifications. These should immediately follow either your contact information or objective (if your objective is short).

Many logical reasons exist for this. First, placing all keywords in one section allows you to keep the rest of your resume the same, avoiding the awkwardness of adding additional keyword phrases throughout the entire resume. Furthermore, you will not have to change the action verbs into nouns. Action verbs read better, but computers most often search nouns. By placing keywords under their own heading, you ensure that the computer will not miss them while keeping the rest of your resume readable for a hiring manager. Additionally, highlighting keywords at the top of your resume allows a manager to scan your resume quickly and to see your qualifications immediately. Another factor is the search properties of some resume retrieval programs. Some programs record only the first 100 keywords, so having them up front rather than scattered throughout is best.

One caveat: do not overdo keywords. Your list should contain 25 keywords or phrases maximum. While employers may feed a program their own arbitrary choice of keywords, 25 keywords and phrases should adequately cover all possibilities.

Interjecting keywords into a resume requires a special skill and talent. However, here are some tips that can help you become proficient.

Read the Want Ads and Job Postings on the Internet

What words does the employer use to advertise the job? In particular, note the industry buzzwords that are used. Compare the ad with others advertising similar positions. Words appearing in all these ads are critical keywords you should use.

Log On to the *Occupational Outlook Handbook* <http://bls.gov/oco/home.htm>

This handbook, produced by the Bureau of Labor Statistics, is an invaluable career reference guide. It lists almost every imaginable job and describes what skills are required. The job descriptions alone contain many crucial keywords. Many of the employers themselves use this guide when writing their ad to recruit new employees.

Scour Trade Journals and Newspaper Articles in Your Field

This will update you on current trends and buzzwords that are becoming popular in your industry.

It cannot be overstressed: *keywords are crucial!* Taking the time and effort to create a master list of keywords for your e-resume is important. You may even want to prepare different sets of keywords to attach to different versions of your e-resume, each geared toward a different area of interest. Additionally, if you use a search engine to scour the Internet for job postings, you will again need your list of industry keywords. Thus, taking the time and ensuring upfront that your list is accurate and complete is worthwhile.

PUTTING TOGETHER A MASTER LIST OF KEYWORDS

You should choose a sampling of keywords that corresponds to each section of your resume. For example, you will want a few keywords to correspond to your objective, specifically an exact job title and description. You will want a group of keywords that represent your "Summary of Qualifications"—how many years of experience you have and marketable personality traits. (See page 6 for a list.) Your experience's keywords should contain all job titles you have held, what skills you have used (see page 5), and industry jargon and buzzwords that apply to your vocation. Key phrases as "increased profits," "reduced operating costs," and other short phrases that summarize your accomplishments without detailing them (see page 49) should represent your achievements. Save the details for the body of your resume. Mentioning the degree you received summarizes your education. Additionally, list certificates, awards, honors, and other pertinent information, such as proficiency in a language or computer programs. The worksheet at the end of this chapter will guide you in preparing a master keyword list.

CAUTION: *Be extra careful to check and double check the spelling of your keywords. Remember if a critical keyword is misspelled, the computer will not read it and your resume may not be selected, all because you interchanged two letters or made some other foolish spelling error.*

Most keyword searches revolve around nouns and descriptive words that characterize your job. For example, if you instructed managers on the use of OCR programs, your main keyword would be the noun "instructor" rather than the verb "instructed." Another keyword from this example would be "OCR programs." Adjectives describing personality traits such as "accurate" and "efficient" are also important to list among your keywords. Of course, make sure that they are relevant to the job at hand.

An Example

The following ad appears in a local paper for an Interior Designer. It reads:

> *Great opportunity for a creative, results-oriented individual who enjoys a team environment. Position requires interior design degree, CAD knowledge, and 7–10 years of experience. We offer an exciting variety of project types, commercial and hospitality.*

In the area of objective, the keyword is simply the job title—Interior Designer. The ad emphasizes "creative" and "team environment," making these specific personality traits keywords—"creative" and "team player." Keywords related to experience would include the number of years of experience the ad calls for (assuming it matches the minimum 7 years required in this specific ad). You would also want to stress your experience in CAD expertise, and experience in commercial design and hospitality design. These keywords are generated directly from the ad itself. Remember, only mention keywords if you can corroborate your experience in these areas and only if your resume supports them.

From the *Occupational Handbook,* you will find the keywords "prepare working drawings," "supervise assistants to carry out the designs," along with many others. This should give you an idea of how to find the keywords for your particular field.

FORMATTING YOUR E-RESUME

The second principal difference in e-resumes affects their design and format rather than their content. Resumes that will be scanned, sent via e-mail, or posted directly to an Internet job board must be designed for the computer. In other words, they must be "computer friendly." While some differences exist between scannable, paper resumes and e-resumes, these formats are converging into one standard e-resume. The rules are basically the same for each.

- *All e-resumes must be in ASCII (plain text).* Scanning programs and many e-mail programs do not perform well with formatted text, even in an "rtf" format (a format read by most word processors). ASCII includes all letters, numbers, and signs on your computer keyboard. *ASCII does not include*
  - bullets or other symbols not on the standard keyboard.
  - any advanced formatting capabilities. This means no bolding, underlining, italics, or even tabs. Indenting should be done with the space bar only.
  - graphics, borders, or shading.
- *Fonts must be simple.* Although true ASCII can support numerous fonts, scanners have a hard time reading many serif fonts and most decorative fonts. Use Courier, Times Roman, Arial, or Universe. These fonts are simple, clean, and easily read by scanners.
- *Fonts should be between 10 point and 14 point.* Do *not* vary font sizes for emphasis. Use only one font and one font size.
- *Length of lines should be limited to 65 characters.* This is the size of a line of text as it appears on a computer monitor. Lines should be broken by using the Return key (a hard line break) rather than relying on automatic word wrapping.
- *All text should be flush left (left justified), including your contact information.*
- *Lists should be indented 3 to 5 spaces, using only the space bar.*
- *The TAB key should not be used because it is not recognized correctly by ASCII.*
- *Margins should be at least one inch on all sides.*
- *The resume must be no longer than two pages, maximum.*
- *Your name should appear on the top of each additional page.*
- *No resume submitted for scanning should be folded or stapled.*
- *To improve the aesthetic look of your resume you can*
  - use all caps in place of boldface. Caps are read by ASCII and can be used to denote the resume headings such as OBJECTIVE and EXPERIENCE.
  - use asterisks (*) or plus signs (+) instead of bullets.
  - use hyphens (-) or double hyphens (--) to signify lists.

CREATING AN E-RESUME ON YOUR WORD PROCESSOR

You should make your formatted resume, replete with boldface, bullets, or underlining with fancy fonts, in an advanced word processor such as Microsoft Word. Then you can simply *convert that resume to ASCII.* Most word processors allow you to easily convert your document into an ASCII version by choosing that option in the save menu of the program. For example, in Word when you select File, then Save As, Word shows you a drop-down menu for Save As Type. This gives you an option to save your file as Text Only, which is a standard ASCII, computer-friendly document. If you must create an e-resume from scratch, you should use Notepad, WordPad (found in Window's Accessories), or any other rudimentary word processor that reads and writes exclusively in ASCII.

Ensure your document is truly computer friendly after saving it (it will have a .txt extension), by e-mailing it to yourself and viewing it—just as an employer would see it. Alternatively, open it in Notepad and see how it looks. Did the line breaks and indenting convert properly? If not, you may have to do some editing in Notepad before saving your finished product. Remember to redo the fonts and font sizes so that they are uniform. You can easily do this by choosing Select All and then changing the font and size. You are now ready to send out your e-resume.

To see two example versions of the same resume, a fully-formatted one and its electronic twin, turn to pages 104 and 105.

E-MAILING YOUR ELECTRONIC RESUME

Sending your resume via e-mail or posting it directly to a job board is a simple task. Once you have your e-resume formatted in ASCII, be sure to save it to a file with a .txt extension. As we mentioned earlier, the simple word-processing programs such as Notepad and WordPad, which come with Windows, are perfect for e-resumes. Then follow the steps below.

1. *Open your e-resume file in the appropriate program.* For example, if your resume is called teacher_1.txt (teacher's resume, version one), and you have saved it in Notepad, open it in Notepad.

2. *Select the entire text.* Either highlight the entire resume, select Edit and then the Select All command, or press CTRL-A.

3. *Copy the text.* Either select Copy in the Edit Menu, or press CTRL-C.

4. *Open your e-mail program and insert your resume.* Position your cursor at the point in your e-mail where you want to insert your resume, and either select Paste from the Edit Menu or press CTRL-V. Alternatively, press Shift-Insert.

EMPLOYERS USUALLY EXPECT YOUR RESUME TO BE IN YOUR E-MAIL, BUT AN EMPLOYER WILL OFTEN REQUEST THAT YOU SEND YOUR RESUME AS AN "ATTACHMENT." THIS MEANS YOUR RESUME IS SENT AS A SEPARATE FILE ATTACHED TO YOUR E-MAIL. IN THIS CASE, THE EMPLOYER MAY EVEN PREFER THAT YOU SEND IT AS A MICROSOFT WORD FILE. IF AN EMPLOYER WANTS THE FILE SENT AS AN ATTACHMENT, YOU MUST FOLLOW THE INSTRUCTIONS FOR YOUR PARTICULAR E-MAIL PROGRAM TO ATTACH THE FILE.

ELECTRONIC COVER LETTERS

Cover letters sent via e-mail or posted on job boards should be treated the same as the resume. They too must adhere to computer-friendly ASCII formatting. However, cover letters you send by regular mail should be formatted. Most resume-tracking software is not used on cover letters; thus, cover letters are generally not scanned. Unfortunately, many experts believe that because these letters are not scanned, they are discarded rather than read. They believe the cover letter may soon be extinct.

Not all experts agree. Many still believe that a well-crafted cover letter is crucial. Numerous employers do not use resume-tracking software, and many who do still read your letter. Others will file your letter to be read later, if the computer selects you as a potential candidate. To be safe, send the best cover letter you can. Frequently, the well-written cover letter determines whether an employer grants you an interview. Furthermore, a cover letter that demonstrates your indispensability to the company will make you truly stand out, something especially vital in today's competitive marketplace.

E-Cover Letters Must Be Concise

All experts agree that cover letters sent via e-mail must be short. Employers receive much e-mail, particularly in response to a job opening, leaving them little time to read a lengthy letter. An e-cover letter *must* cut to the chase. It should not be an attachment, but rather should be pasted (in ASCII) into the body of your e-mail. It should serve only as an introduction to your attached e-resume. In your e-cover letter you should

↪ *state the job for which you are applying.*

↪ *tell the employer where you heard about the opening.* If someone the employer knows recommended you, be sure to mention that person's name.

↪ *state that you possess all the required qualifications, which the employer will find documented in your enclosed resume.*

Then *end it!* Skip a few lines, insert your e-resume into the body of the e-mail, and send it. If the employer has asked for your resume as an attachment, end your e-cover letter, attach your resume, and send them together.

HAVE A MORE DETAILED COVER LETTER READY TO SEND THE EMPLOYER IF HE OR SHE SHOWS ANY INTEREST. YOU CAN MAIL THIS LONGER VERSION LATER OR SEND IT VIA A SECOND E-MAIL AFTER THE EMPLOYER HAS CONTACTED YOU. YOU MAY EVEN WANT TO SEND IT AS A FOLLOW-UP AFTER AN INTERVIEW. IN THIS COVER LETTER YOU SHOULD BE MORE DETAILED AND MORE SPECIFIC. ITS PURPOSE IS TO DEMONSTRATE AND EMPHASIZE YOUR ABILITIES AS A "PROBLEM SOLVER." TO PREPARE THIS COVER LETTER, CAREFULLY READ CHAPTER 13.

THE PROFESSIONAL PORTFOLIO—THE RESUME COMPANION

The proliferation of computers and inexpensive desktop publishing programs has opened new opportunities that were once too expensive for the jobseeker. One area in particular that is becoming more popular among job seekers, especially college graduates, is creating a professional portfolio to showcase your abilities.

The professional portfolio is designed to be a *companion* to your resume. A portfolio is simply a collection of samples of one's work. Previously, only artists, models, and others in the creative arts used portfolios to showcase their talents. Artists would bring large attaché cases to their interviews containing samples of their paintings or graphic designs. Models and actors would carry an ensemble of photos to present their many poses and "faces." Quite recently the idea of a portfolio has reached almost every occupational field. Today's professionals find value in a portfolio containing their resume, letters of reference, samples of their work, records of their accomplishments, papers they have written or published, or any other documents that substantiate the benefits they have to offer an employer. While a resume lists skills, a portfolio demonstrates them in a concrete way. When skillfully planned and organized, the portfolio can be an invaluable instrument for getting a job.

Many colleges and trade schools are encouraging their students to assemble portfolios that exhibit a variety of the student's work, achievements, and recognition. Letters from instructors and student projects are important for an employer to see. For the graduating student who has little job experience, this can be crucial.

WHAT SHOULD YOUR PORTFOLIO CONTAIN?

Think of your portfolio as an expanded version of your resume. Just as with your resume, everything in your portfolio must relate to your objective. Do not add anything artsy, cute, or irrelevant to your career objective. Hobbies, clubs, and family photographs do not belong in your professional portfolio. Only material that supports your objective and resume belongs.

Your portfolio should mirror your resume. You list work experience in your resume; thus in your portfolio you should include documents or letters of recommendation that emphasize your experience. Try to document any concrete results for which you were personally responsible. Just as demonstrating your skills and accomplishments is the goal of your resume, your portfolio should do the same. Again, include items that demonstrate employer benefits. Just as your resume highlights certificates and awards, your portfolio can contain the actual documents and awards you have received. In short, anything that supports your career objective and demonstrates your ability should be in your portfolio.

Checklist for a Professional Portfolio

- ☐ Resume
- ☐ Written samples of work (published articles, project outlines)
- ☐ Photos of projects
- ☐ Charts and graphs that demonstrate success
- ☐ Other materials that support your objective
- ☐ Licenses and certificates
- ☐ Awards (employers' or teachers' evaluation reports)
- ☐ Letters of praise from superiors or instructors
- ☐ Letters of recommendation

HOW TO USE YOUR PORTFOLIO

Several ways exist to utilize your portfolio; though primarily you will use it during the interview.

Once a company is interested in you and calls about an interview, bring your portfolio along to the interview. At this stage, the company is interested in knowing everything about you, and if your portfolio shines, it may earn you the job. You can also use it as a blueprint for a dedicated Web page. Online resumes are becoming more popular, and they are simply an electronic portfolio. Moreover, downloading your "electronic portfolio" on CD, allows you to send by mail to a prospective manager easily. You can even indicate in your cover letter (or resume) "Portfolio available upon request." The idea is to have it readily available.

THE JOB SEARCH PORTFOLIO

Another type of portfolio is a more personal one. It is organized to help you, the job seeker, and is for your eyes only. It is basically a collection of job search materials, which you should always have available. Using a three-ring binder and appropriate dividers will best accomplish this. Inside will be

- ↪ all versions of your resume, numbered or coded to document which version was sent to which employer, on which date. Make a note in the calendar section when a follow-up call is due to that party.
- ↪ a record of each cover letter you sent.

- a copy or printout of every want ad or online job post that you answered.

- industry information, such as articles from trade journals, periodicals, or printouts from Internet sites, which will help prepare you for an interview.

- company research information from all sources.

- names, phone numbers, and addresses of people who you have contacted in the job search.

- a detailed journal of results from the job search—rejections, interviews, and follow-ups.

- a calendar with follow-up phone call and interview dates recorded.

- a "To Do" page, preferably at the beginning of the notebook, where you list on a daily basis what tasks must be done for the job search, and then check them off when they are accomplished.

Keeping a Job Portfolio or journal is imperative. You will send out many resumes and talk to many people, making it difficult to balance your priorities. Especially in today's electronic market, so many resumes are e-mailed and job posts answered that keeping an updated, detailed journal is vital.

In Chapter 19 you will find Your Personal Job Journal. These pages can be removed from your workbook and placed in a binder. Make copies of any pages that you think you will fill and have them handy. These pages will form the foundation of your Job Search Portfolio.

If you prefer, use a personal-information-manager (PIM) computer program to store your information. Programs such as Outlook will allow you to keep a calendar and all your contact information in one place. Many free e-mail sites, such as Yahoo!, now offer calendars as well. If you have access to a scanner, you can scan all relevant newspaper and journal articles and keep them with downloaded Web pages for easy retrieval. However, *make a backup and hard copy printout of all information.* If your computer crashes, all your vital and irreplaceable information could be lost.

WEB RESUMES: YOUR PERSONAL WEB PAGE RESUME

Two ways exist to transform your resume into its own unique Web page. The simplest way is to transfer the beautifully formatted version of your resume onto its own Web page. Employers who receive your e-resume and want to see your formatted version, can easily log onto your Web site for a look. Most word processors allow you to save a file in HTML (the Web page standard), which means creating a Web page dedicated to your formatted resume is as simple as saving your file in HTML and then uploading it to your Web page. If you formatted your resume in MS Word or any other popular program, creating your Web page will take only a few minutes.

If you are already creating a dedicated Web page, take advantage of the available features. You can add graphics, and sound, and links to your main page, transforming your Web resume into a Web "portfolio." You can organize your Web page exactly as you would your portfolio.

One link can take the reader to letters of recommendation; another link to research papers or projects that you can scan into the computer. You can link graphs, graphics, pictorials, and almost anything else from your page.

Advantages of a Web Page Resume

Besides the advantage of creating a more aesthetically pleasing resume, one that uses graphics and other media forms to stand out, a Web resume offers other benefits.

↬ *You can password protect your site.* Password protecting specific pages, or your entire site, allows you to control how much of your Web resume various people can view.

↬ *You can have a potential employer access your Web page during an interview.* An employer who has access to the Web can open your portfolio during the interview, and you can conduct a tour that highlights your skills and accomplishments. Thus, you are actually using your Web site as a portfolio.

↬ *You can interview with an employer on the phone.* You can show an employer around your Web site as he or she talks to your from their office and views your Web page on a monitor.

↬ *You can download your Web page onto a disk or CD and send it to an employer.* You can do this either before or after the interview. The employer will have something to review even after you have left the interview. It also allows the employer to show your work to other colleagues who may be involved in the hiring process. Additionally, downloading your Web page portfolio to a disk is an inexpensive alternative to sending costly portfolios to each employer.

If you do maintain a Web site, hyperlink to it. You can place the hyperlink directly in your contact information (on your letterhead) under your phone number and e-mail address, or you can even include it in your e-mail signature. Thus, an interested employer can immediately access your Web site, allowing you to hold their attention. A well-executed Web site with striking visuals and graphics is another tool that helps you stand above the competition.

CREATING A DEDICATED RESUME WEB SITE

The actual creation of a Web site is beyond the scope of this book. One obviously has to have the proper software program and follow the instructions in the program's manual. Some Web browsers offer "lite" software versions to create Web pages. More elaborate programs can be purchased at any local software outlet. Additional programs containing libraries of graphics and clip art can also be purchased everywhere. The costs can run high. Many people with limited backgrounds in HTML have found it more cost effective to hire a college student to prepare their Web resume. Remember, if you maintain a Web site that everyone can access, it had better look good!

MULTIMEDIA RESUMES

Another recent development in resume writing (which evolved from the Web site resume) is multimedia resumes. These can be resumes with video images, sound, graphics, or any other multimedia accouterments. They can be sent on discs as well. They can range from simple programs created with presentation software such as Microsoft PowerPoint to complex short video presentations utilizing video footage.

Many tools are now available to an individual that only a few years ago were either unheard of or costly beyond reason. These techniques allow individuals to use their creativity in presenting themselves in a far more effective way than with a traditional resume. Integrating these new approaches with older, more traditional job search methods can generate outstanding results.

WORKSHEET INSTRUCTIONS

This worksheet may be the most important one you will complete. Choosing the right keywords is *crucial* because without them, a computer will not select your resume regardless of your qualifications. Furthermore, keywords will become the focus in successful Web engine searches when you scour the Web for job opportunities.

Therefore, take time now to generate a solid list of keywords.

Your keywords should represent each area of your resume. To help you select effective keywords, use the skill lists on pages 4–6, the action verbs on page 43, and the accomplishments on page 49. Remember that nouns and adjectives are more commonly used in search programs. Additionally, use the want ads and online job postings to find keywords and buzzwords that employers are using. You may want to access the *Occupational Outlook Handbook* as well.

First, select *all the keywords* that you believe apply to your objective. All keywords should support *one objective.* If you are seeking multiple jobs, make a *separate list for each objective.*

After you have selected a "master list," go through the list and *circle the 25 best keywords.* Include these in your e-resume.

CHAPTER 16 / WORKSHEET

Electronic Resumes

Resume Area:	Keywords:	
OBJECTIVE (Job titles and technical skill areas)		
QUALIFICATIONS (Personality traits, years of experience)		
SKILLS		
ACHIEVEMENTS (success words)		
RESPONSIBILITES & TASKS		
LICENSES & CERTIFICATES		

(continued)

CHAPTER 16 / WORKSHEET (continued)

Electronic Resumes

Resume Area:	Keywords:
COMPUTER SKILLS	
EDUCATION	
KEYWORDS FROM ADS	
OCCUPATIONAL HANDBOOK <http://bls.gov/oco/home.htm>	
TRADE JOURNALS	
BLUEMOND'S *WORD FINDER*	

CHAPTER 17

NETWORKING

UNCOVERING THE HIDDEN JOB MARKET

What Is Networking?

According to experts, more than 80 percent of all available jobs are *not* in the want ads nor are the numerous employment agencies aware of them. Some of these hidden jobs may open due to company expansion, or employees that retire or change jobs; others exist because of the development of new products. How do you learn about and apply for these openings?

The answer is *networking*. Networking means seeking out personal contacts who can give you the names of potential employers, or better yet, put you directly in touch with them. Networking means contacting everyone you know who can give you referrals; friends, relatives, acquaintances, coworkers, professional organization members—anyone who can give you the names of people who are hiring.

Remember, most people land their jobs from personal references, not from employment agencies or want ads. However, you must work at it. You must take initiative; control your own future. You cannot be passive and wait for an employment agency to call or a want ad to appear. You must create opportunities.

Networking is a method of job search by which you build up a body of support people (secondary contacts) who will ultimately put you in contact with potential employers (primary contacts). These primary contacts become your target market—the people you will send your resume to and contact for interviews.

Through networking, you discover which companies are hiring and which person (at each company) is in charge of the process. Your next step is to directly contact that person (not personnel) and ask for an interview. To obtain a job you must reach the person in charge of hiring and meet him or her. Networking will help you get there.

DEVELOPING A LIST OF CONTACTS

The first step in achieving your goal is to build a repertoire of primary contacts—names of people or organizations who are looking to hire someone with your skills and background.

Two methods for generating such a list are networking (asking people to assist you) and research (scouring trade journals, newspapers, and yellow pages for leads). The Internet has become a major source of networking, too, as was discussed in Chapter 15.

151

Start by asking coworkers or other professionals in your field if they know who is looking to hire. College classmates, alumni, college placement offices, and bankers are also good sources to ask. Friends and relatives may also know people who can help you. Do not be shy—ask everyone for names of people that can help you. Sometimes a friend will give you the name of another friend who in turn will give you someone else to call. Keep calling and keep getting names of more contacts.

Always keep a list of who referred you to whom. When you call your contacts, mention the name of the person who referred you to them. Many times this personal connection will help break the ice and get you in the door, especially if the contact respects your referrer's judgment.

The best contacts are those who will personally intercede on your behalf and tell an employer about you. Although these contacts are uncommon, they can still help you build a solid list of names of primary contacts you can call yourself.

Call every name on your list. If the people you have been referred to cannot help you, ask them for the names of people they know who can. It is a numbers game—the more names you get, the better your chances are of finding an employer who will hire you.

THE INFORMATIONAL INTERVIEW

One of the most effective networking techniques is the informational interview. Unlike a job interview, this is an interview you arrange with someone influential in your field; someone who can help you. The purpose of the interview is two-fold.

↪ You will get information and professional advice from an expert in the field.

↪ You will add an important contact to your network—one who may help you find a good job.

Is there someone in your field you have heard or read about that could help you? Contact them. Is there a business for which you would like to work? Contact the person who has the authority to hire you, even though you know that no jobs are presently open. *Make it clear to this person at the start that you are not asking for a job.* Explain that you are entering the field and the purpose of your call is to set up a short meeting (15 minutes) to get his or her professional advice. Most people will be flattered that you want their advice and will meet with you.

At the meeting, stress again that you are not asking for a job, but for advice. Ask for details about the job you would like to do. Determine what sort of experience is necessary. Learn what sort of problems come with the job and what is expected of an employee. Tell the contact about your background. Ask the person what he or she believes is the best job search strategy for someone in your position. Listen to the advice. At the end of the meeting thank the contact for his or her time.

Before you leave, ask your contact two key questions.

1. Ask if you can leave a copy of your resume—in case something opens.

2. Ask if they know of someone at another company who could use somebody with your background and qualifications.

Calling someone at another company and using your new influential contact as a referral can open otherwise closed doors!

Immediately upon getting home, follow up the meeting with a thank-you note. Then keep in touch with your contact. Call approximately every six weeks to see if he or she has any news for you.

The informational interview is one of the most effective methods of networking. The interview will give you important information about the job you are seeking, as well as put you in direct contact with someone influential—someone who can intercede on your behalf, which is the best possible contact.

RESEARCH

Research is another method for procuring a list of primary contacts. Read the local business section in the newspaper to see which companies are expanding or opening new branches. Remember, every organization in your field (or one that uses people in your field) is a potential employer.

To find the names of organizations and potential employers in your industry use the following resources:

↱ Yellow Pages

↱ industry trade journals

↱ newspaper business section

↱ state and city directories

↱ *Standard & Poor's* (http://www.standardandpoors.com)

↱ *Dun & Bradstreet* (http://www.dnb.com)

Many states have directories listing all major corporations and organizations conducting business in their state. Most of these directories categorize the businesses by industry, making them a useful source for building a contact list. Always get both the name of the organization and that of the person in charge of hiring. If you can only get the name of the organization, call it. Ask a secretary or an assistant for the name of the person in charge of the department that interests you. Get his or her name and write it down—do not talk to that person yet. Waiting until you research the company is best, because you will be calling that person without a referral. Be prepared with information before you make your initial contact.

WHAT ABOUT THE WANT ADS?

Never make the want ads a priority. Most want ads generate so many resumes that yours can easily get lost in the shuffle. Some experts suggest looking in old newspapers and answering last month's want ads. If the ad is no longer running, the chances of new resumes coming in will be slim. If the job is still available (which is very likely), your chances for getting it are increased. With few resumes arriving, yours will get attention.

If the hiring company's name does not appear in the want ad, be leery. The want ad may be phony. An employment agency looking to increase its resume bank may have placed the ad. Alternatively, a company who has no job opening but wants to see who the competition is and check out who is in the marketplace may have placed it. A company may also have placed it as a legal formality, even though it already knows whom it plans to hire. If there is no company name, be suspicious and avoid it. Begin with reputable companies that are hiring.

Perhaps the best use of the want ads is as a source for adding primary contacts to your network list. Directly call those companies and get the name of the person in charge of hiring. Contact that person directly, overstepping personnel.

This does not mean that you should never answer a want ad, however never consider them a number one priority. Use your best judgment. Always concentrate your effort on personal contacts.

TELEPHONE YOUR CONTACTS

Once you have a list of organizations and businesses who need people with your background and skills, set aside time each day to call. Call every one of these organizations! Find out if there are any openings available. If nothing is presently open, ask what future plans the company has. Get information. Additionally, get the name of the person who, if a job opening occurred, would be in charge of hiring. Write down his or her name and title for future reference. This is the person you will call in the future to ask about work or to set up an informational interview.

Do research. Learn everything you can about the companies that interests you. Develop a strategy. What could you do for them if you were hired?

When you have a clear idea of how you could contribute to a company, it is time to call the person in charge of the department that interests you. Tell them about yourself and give them an idea (do not tell them everything) of what you believe that you could do for them. Ask them for an interview, or at least if you could send them your resume. If you can impress the employers enough, or arouse their curiosity, you may just get an interview (and a job) even though nothing is presently open.

KEEP A JOURNAL

It cannot be overstressed: *always keep an updated journal*. Record each employer who expresses an interest in you on your master list. This is your target market. In your journal, record all of your activities. Note if you send an employer a resume or other correspondence. Do the same for all phone calls and meetings. Record the date and the outcome of each, and always follow up.

As mentioned in Chapter 16, the journal can be part of your Job Search Portfolio or in a computer PIM program, such as Outlook or Act.

FOLLOW UP

Give your contact approximately one week to receive your resume or cover letter and to review it. Then follow up. Call and ask if he or she received your resume. Tell him or her that you are looking forward to meeting in person at a possible interview. Be polite, but be firm. If he or she tells you that the position has been filled or that you will not be interviewed, ask your favorite question: Do you know anyone else who would be interested in someone with my background?

Never relent until you get a job. Even if a job is not presently available, call your target employers every month to check on the situation. Make sure they still remember you. Thus, if a job opens, they will consider you.

Keep adding to your contacts and always follow up. Persistence is crucial. Thomas Edison famously said, "Genius is 1 percent inspiration and 99 percent perspiration."

THE JOB INTERVIEW

PRE-INTERVIEW PREPARATION

The Interview Gets You the Job

The interview is the most important component of the job search process. While your resume and cover letter get you the interview, the interview, and how well you perform during it, ultimately gets you the job. Usually, many candidates are interviewed and how well you outperform the competition will determine the final outcome. How you present yourself and the image you project will be crucial factors in getting the job you want.

Your resume documents your skills and accomplishments, yet this is usually insufficient. How you interact with your employer and coworkers is even more important. A major objective of the interview is to unmask your true personality and to demonstrate your ability to work with others. While you cannot control the chemistry an employer may have with a candidate, one thing is true: the more you prepare for the interview, the more you will impress the employer and increase your chances he or she will hire you.

You *Can* Create Chemistry

Researching the company and job is vital. If you understand the skills employers are looking for and the image they expect from their employees, you can create that all-important chemistry.

Employers want to believe that your primary motive for seeking work with them is not just the paycheck. They want to be convinced that the company's reputation excites you and makes you want to work there. If you can convey such enthusiasm, chemistry will follow.

RESEARCHING THE COMPANY, THE JOB, AND THE EMPLOYER IS YOUR KEY TO CREATING A FAVORABLE IMPRESSION, A PROFESSIONAL IMAGE, AND ULTIMATELY A GOOD CHEMISTRY BETWEEN YOU AND THE EMPLOYER.

What an Employer Looks For

An employer will consider two basic questions. Foremost, do you have the skills and experience required for the job? Subsequently, are you the type of person the company wants to employ? To decide the latter, the employer looks for two qualities. First, what is your sense of business ethics—are you honest, reliable, and dependable, or will you frequently call in sick and leave after two months? Second, will you integrate well with your fellow workers, get along with the employer, and be enthusiastic about the company and your job?

The employer uses the interview to get an overall picture of you in order to gauge how well you will fit into the company. Most interview questions will focus on the following issues.

Substantiate Your Resume

You claim you have the skills required, now prove it! The interviewer will probe and ask questions to verify that your resume is not exaggerated or inflated. You may be asked detailed technical questions or how you might handle a specific problem that would be part of your job. You will be asked to expand on statements in your resume and to give concrete examples. You may even be given a written skill test during or prior to the interview. Additionally, many employers may opt for a "cast interview" (discussed later in this chapter) to see how well you use your skills to solve speculative problems that you may encounter on the job. Questions about your education may also be raised. Be prepared to talk about what you wrote in your resume and to furnish details, as well as to demonstrate your problem-solving skills on the spot.

"Check Out" Your Personality

You will be asked questions about past employers, how well you got along with them, why you left your last job, and how you handle stress. You may be asked how you think your last employer will talk about you and how many days you were absent during the past year. The object is to determine that you are hardworking, ethical, and able to work well with others. Again, psychometric tests may be given to determine if your personality is a fit for the job at hand. Therefore, do your research and be prepared.

Assess Your Value and Determine Your Salary

The employer wants to know that your contributions to the organization will be greater than the cost of hiring you. Although you should never bring up the question of salary (especially on a first interview), be prepared to negotiate if the employer brings up the issue. Know the accepted salary range for your position before going into the interview. Clarify benefits, vacation time, and working conditions, if the issues are raised. Unfortunately, accepting a lower salary is sometimes a major factor in getting the job. Decide on the lowest salary you will accept if the job is offered on the spot, but always try to negotiate higher or for more benefits.

How to Sell Yourself

Everything you do during the interview will be noticed. Not only what you say, but how you say it. If you fidget and seem uncomfortable or if you are uncertain of yourself, the interviewer will observe it. Be confident, give it your all, and most important, try to control the interview to your advantage, accentuating the benefits you have to offer.

The focus of your answers should demonstrate your ability to solve problems. Try to illustrate how you would perform on the job. Prove to the employer that he or she should hire you rather than another candidate.

Again, preparation is the key to selling yourself. You must research the company and job so that you clearly understand how your skills can solve company problems.

Do research to identify the specific problems you may encounter on the job. During the interview, impress the employer with your knowledge of the company and convince him or her that you can solve the problems that the job may entail.

Show the employer that you have done your homework. Many applicants will go into the interview knowing very little about the prospective company. Speaking knowledgably about the organization and conveying enthusiasm for the job will put you ahead of most. However, be careful of overkill. Offering too much information with the intent to impress can make you come across as an obnoxious know-it-all.

Stress the employer benefits you have to offer: increasing sales, saving money, increasing proficiency, or any other benefits or accomplishments listed in Chapters 5 and 7. Illustrate your skills and abilities with stories and examples from your past work history (in particular those documented in your resume). Establish yourself as a respected and serious worker. Bring a list of references and testimonials or letters of recommendation if you have them.

Most important, display your willingness to work with others and fit into the company's image. Talk to people in the industry (employees of the firm if you can) to discover the expected image. Dress and act accordingly.

How to Research a Company

Talking with current employees is the best way to research a firm. Try to set up a meeting with an employee. You probably can meet some employees by frequenting their favorite cafeteria or you may just call cold. Introduce yourself and explain that you have been chosen to be interviewed for a position in their company and would like some information. Inviting them to lunch may put them more at ease. Learn as much as you can about the company, the job, and the interviewer (employer). Be sure to thank the employee. He or she may even put in a good word for you. The Internet has become an invaluable resource for conducting pre-interview research. Refer to Chapter 15 for more information on using the Web for research.

Other useful resources are

➝ employees of competitive firms.

➝ annual reports.

➝ company newsletters.

➝ local business journals.

➝ Polk's city directories.

➝ state directories.

➝ directory of corporate affiliations.

➝ *Who's Who In* . . . books.

Ask your librarian for more assistance if you need it. Many of these resources can also be accessed on the Web.

TYPES OF INTERVIEWS

In today's workforce, various interview formats are standard. Rising costs of training and keeping employees has made most companies cautious about hiring the right person. Consequently, more sophisticated interview techniques are becoming common. Familiarizing yourself with the various types of interview and question formats that you are likely to encounter in your job search is important.

Serial Interview

Candidates undergo a series of interviews. The initial interview is relatively simple and is intended primarily to screen out unqualified applicants. The first round of questions is geared at determining the technical qualifications and abilities of the candidate. If an applicant passes the first interview, he or she has a second, more intense interview. A variety of leading questions will be used to uncover the applicant's personality and ability to be a team player. Serial interviews are common for positions of responsibility and authority, especially managerial jobs.

Sequential Interview

The candidate undergoes a series of interviews, only this time a different interviewer conducts each interview. The purpose is to have many interviewers judge the candidate. The decision to hire will be a group decision based upon the opinion of all those who interviewed the applicant. This method of interview is frequently used for a position that requires the employee to interact with multiple people. Each of the potential co-bosses may interview the candidate.

Panel Interview

A panel, rather than one interviewer, questions the applicant. The panel will usually consist of people whom the candidate will be responsible to if he or she gets the job. The panel interview serves the same purpose as the sequential interview, but all interviewers are present simultaneously.

Group Interview

Although rarely used, in this method two or more candidates are interviewed together by one or more interviewers. This method is employed to compare the applicants face-to-face and often used to see which one will exert a leadership role over the others.

INTERVIEW FORMATS

Structured Interview

Each candidate is asked a series of pre-selected questions. All candidates are asked the same questions, allowing the interviewer to compare their answers easily. The upcoming sections list many frequently asked questions and explain how to answer them effectively.

Unstructured Interview

Candidates speak freely about their past work history and accomplishments, usually from their resume. The interviewer will form an overall (subjective) picture about each candidate.

Stress Interview

This format is also called *targeted selection interviewing*. The interviewer asks deeply probing questions to determine how well the candidate handles him or herself. Leading questions may be asked to analyze the candidate's decision-making process, and to try to make the applicant uncomfortable and unbalanced just to see the reaction. These questions are usually unexpected and the type the candidate could not have prepared for in advance, such as "What's the worse thing you've heard about our company?" "What's the worst mistake you made on your last job?" "Why did it happen?" "Whose fault was it?" (Will you blame your employer or coworkers, or will you accept the blame yourself?)

In this situation, the best strategy is *always remain calm*. Moreover, never retract what you have previously stated. Many employers want to see if you are indecisive and easily persuaded. Be calm, firm, and always exude confidence.

Behavioral Interview

Like the stress interview, the behavioral interview asks more intimidating questions that will probe your problem-solving abilities. The interviewer will ask a series of questions that require you to describe how you actually handled difficult situations. Rather than asking "what would you do if," the interviewer will ask "what *did* you do *when*." Recounting specific examples from the past offers the employer a good predictor for future performance.

For example, rather than ask you how you would deal with a coworker who was difficult to get along with, the employer may say, "Give me an example of a situation where you had to deal with a difficult coworker and how you handled it." Other such questions you may encounter are

- ↪ Give an example of a time when you had to make a decision but did not have all the necessary information. What did you do?
- ↪ What was the most difficult customer-service situation you had to handle?
- ↪ What is the most significant contribution you made to your past employer?
- ↪ When was the last time you were criticized on the job? How did you respond? What did you learn from the situation?

Preparing for probing questions such as these is not easy. If asked about a situation you never experienced on the job, you may, in that case, offer a "hypothetical" answer and explain what you would do if you were to encounter such a problem. You should always remain calm and think clearly. Speak with confidence and enthusiasm. Often an employer will just want to see how you react under stress. How you carry yourself can be equally or more important than the actual response. Enthusiasm, an upbeat disposition, and confidence are of utmost importance.

Case Interview

Case interviews are especially popular in marketing and consulting firms. A case interview is one in which the candidate is presented with a case or problem similar to one you would encounter on the job and you must analyze and answer on the spot. The employer is checking your analytic reasoning skills, your ability to conceptualize, your attention to detail, your creativity, and especially your ability to communicate your ideas precisely. Often, math and other technical skills will be necessary to solve the case.

Whereas a resume and even an interview may result in the candidate offering information that is inaccurate, the case interview is always truthful. It shows the employer exactly what analytic thinking tools you are equipped with and is an indication of how you will perform on the job.

Some case interviews may involve simple brainteasers to evaluate your reasoning skills. An example may be: You have 2 empty bottles. One holds 3 cups, the other holds 5. How do you get exactly 4 cups of water from the sink?

Others can be more complicated. For example, a candidate may be asked: How many boxes of detergent were sold in St. Louis last year? Here the test is to see if you can make logical assumptions, do simple calculations, and draw logical conclusions. You may explain that there are approximately 350,000 people in St. Louis. If the average household has five members, there are 70,000 households. If each household does four loads of laundry a week and uses detergent which gives you 40 loads to a box, each family will use one box of detergent in ten weeks or approximately five to six boxes per year. If you multiply these five boxes per year times the 70,000 households, it results in approximately 350,000 boxes of detergent sold in St. Louis in one year. Usually it's not the correct answer that matters, but rather the method and thinking used to arrive at the conclusion.

Although preparing for such an interview is virtually impossible, there are some considerations to remember when being confronted with a case interview.

- Identify key concepts.
- Separate important facts from irrelevant ones.
- Make *reasonable* assumptions.
- Look for creative approaches or new insights to solving a problem.
- Communicate your ideas clearly and enthusiastically.

Telephone Interview and E-Mail Interview

To reduce costs, many hiring managers are now conducting their initial screening of applicants via interviews administered by phone or e-mail. In a phone interview, the employer simply asks the applicant a list of rudimentary questions during a short phone call. The e-mail interview operates the same way. Instead of a phone call, the applicant receives an e-mail from an employer asking him to elaborate on items mentioned in his resume or to answer a list of short questions, which he then e-mails back to the employer. Both of these methods are used to evaluate candidates before inviting a selected few for a personal interview. These short interviews save the company time and money spent on unqualified applicants who can be eliminated with a simple phone call or e-mail.

For the job applicant, a marked difference exists between e-mail interviews and those conducted over the phone. In answering an e-mail, you have time to think about the questions and to formulate answers carefully before sending them back. In a phone interview, you have to answer immediately. A phone call can come at an inconvenient time, so you must always be ready. Remember that your phone interview may be recorded and played back to others involved in the hiring process.

Keeping your "job search portfolio" by the phone is a good strategy. Minimally, have your resume and research notes pertaining to each company easily accessible. Do not get flustered; try to answer each question with confidence. If you have a dedicated Web page resume, you may suggest that the interviewer open your Web page while you "walk him or her through it." Again, as the market becomes more competitive, these "pre-interview" methods are becoming more popular.

Computer-Assisted Job Interviews

Computer-assisted job interviews are also gaining popularity due to the time and money saved by having an applicant answer multiple choice or true and false interview questions administered by a computer. This can be done at a computer station set up within the company or sometimes in one's home over the Internet. Some computer-assisted interviews are even being conducted by phone. A prerecorded message asks numerous interview questions, which the applicant answers by punching the proper digit on a touch-tone pad.

These computer interviews usually include questions about your employment history, skills, education, and even your work ethics and personal traits. Many of the tests are timed and the computer will flag questions that took an unusually long time to answer. Studies have shown that people who are lying or trying to rationalize an inaccurate answer will spend an unusually long time answering.

A computer-assisted interview holds many advantages for the applicant, too. Most people are less self-conscious and nervous in front of the computer. The computer is not biased, so your score is the same regardless of gender or race. All applicants answer the same questions, so an employer can more easily make comparisons between them. The computer can summarize skill levels, flag inconsistencies between answers, note unusually long pauses, and sometimes suggest follow-up questions the employer can ask a candidate at a second interview conducted by a human.

Similarly, many companies are also administrating computerized personality tests and skill-level tests to assist them in evaluating the suitability of a candidate, as mentioned in Chapter 14. Today, firing an individual can result in discrimination lawsuits and other expensive legal entailments, so employers are taking every possible precaution to evaluate individuals before hiring them.

THE INTERVIEW

Getting Ready for the Interview

Be sure you are clear on the date, time, and location of your interview. It cannot be stressed enough. In excitement, some people forget to make a note of the date or time and quickly forget. *Immediately write the date, time, and place in your notebook.* If possible, find out the name of the person who will be conducting the interview and write it down.

If you are unsure of the address, ask directions. Do not bother the employer, but call the company later and ask one of the secretaries or assistants for directions. Be clear on how long it will take you to arrive. Arriving late to an interview can be disastrous.

When you do your research before the interview, make notes on a copy of your resume. Bring that copy with you to the interview. Most interviewers will not object to your using your resume during the interview. Often during the stress of the interview, you may forget key dates or key issues you want to cover, so having your resume and notes on hand is helpful.

Be sure to bring three or four extra copies of your resume to the interview. The interviewer may need one, and may want to distribute copies to others. Additionally, bring your references (see Chapter 11), letters of recommendation, testimonials, and if applicable, samples of your work. If you have a business card, bring some along. Furthermore, bring a pad and pen to take notes in case the interviewer gives you information to write down. Carry everything in a professional-looking briefcase or portfolio.

Dress for Success

Dressing in proper attire is crucial. A candidate's overall appearance will make a lasting impression on the interviewer. Your appearance at an interview may not get you the job, but the wrong attire can lose you the job. In dressing for an interview, dress in accordance with the style of clothes worn by current employees. Accounting and finance firms may expect their personnel to wear suits in conservative colors. Advertising firms and other creative areas may be more accepting of a casual style. Learn what sort of attire is expected of you and dress accordingly. If you are unsure, err on the conservative side. Additionally, looking at brochures and the Web site of a prospective employer will probably help you in choosing your garb.

More conservative firms usually prefer men in business suits in a neutral color such as gray, blue, or charcoal, made of a natural fiber (wool or wool blends). Wear a pressed, white shirt with a tie. A professionally laundered shirt is always best. Additionally, wear dark socks and dress shoes. Do not try to make a fashion statement; the idea is to present a professional, successful image. Most companies are very particular about the image they and their workers project, and you must fit in to work there.

Many businesses today are dressing more casually. Casual for a man would mean a sports coat and dress slacks or khakis. However, jeans, shorts, T-shirts, caps, hiking boots, and other gym wear is frowned upon. An employer may feel that if you do not care enough to dress in proper attire for an interview, you will not respect the company and the job. Again, always err toward the conservative side in dress.

For women, conservative clothing translates into something modest, such as a skirted suit made of natural fiber, cut in a classic style. A silk blouse is recommended if you can afford it. For shoes, a classic pump is best. Stay away from flashy clothes. For women, casual wear would include pantsuits, khakis, and cardigan twin sets. Whatever you wear, you should remember your goal is to present a professional image. Dress in an attractive manner, but do not overdo it. If an interviewer remembers your outfit most, you may have made a fashion statement at the expense of a job.

Men and women should both be careful not to wear too much jewelry. Furthermore, do not use too much aftershave or perfume. A strong scent that is unpleasant to the interviewer or one that may cause an allergic reaction can adversely affect your interview. If you are a smoker, be sure your clothes do not smell like smoke. Women should also be careful not to overdo their makeup. Although these rules are not official, the key is to wear clothing that fits in with the job at hand and does not stand out.

Come to the interview freshly bathed and groomed. Men should trim beards and mustaches, or shave. Both men and women should opt for conservative hairstyles (short hair preferred). Use deodorant, brush your teeth, and be sure your nails are clean. The interviewer will consciously and subconsciously take *everything* into account. Present a conservative and professional image and you will be fine.

Arriving at the Interview

Arrive five or ten minutes early if possible. However, do not arrive earlier than that. Employers tend to get nervous when an applicant is sitting around waiting to be interviewed. If an unsuspected emergency occurs and you will be late, call the employer. He or she may want to reschedule your interview.

Come in rested and mentally prepared. Do not drink alcohol before the interview. Do not smoke in the waiting room and certainly not during the interview. Turn off your cell phone during an interview. Spend time reviewing your resume and readying yourself for the interview. Wait until the interviewer introduces himself or herself and offers his or her hand, before offering yours. Never use the interviewer's first name unless told to do so, and wait for instructions before taking a seat.

THE QUESTIONS

What to Expect

Questions will cover the following areas:

↝ education
↝ work experience
↝ career goals

- personality and motivation
- reasons for changing jobs
- stress questions
- salary and benefits

The employer has specific worries about hiring you and will use the interview to dispel these fears. The major ones include:

- Do you require constant supervision?
- Are you only interested in the paycheck?
- How well will you get along with coworkers?
- Will your social life affect your job?
- Do you use your time productively?
- Will you be loyal to the company?
- Are you honest and reliable?
- Will you be content with the salary and working conditions?

Once you recognize the motivation behind the questions, your answers can help dispel the employer's fears. Always present yourself as a problem solver, energetic, willing to work hard, and someone who fits in with the company culture. If you make it clear that you love your work and are willing to work hard, you will be a top candidate for the job.

Tips on Answering Questions

First and foremost, *never lie*. According to the Burke Marketing survey, lying and dishonesty rank as the number one trait employers find the most objectionable. Even if you were fired from a previous job, do not conceal it. If asked details, explain what happened but qualify it. Tell the employer what you learned from the experience and why it will never happen again. Remember, most employers will check candidates before hiring them, so do not lie to make yourself look better—it could cost you the job.

Always make eye contact. Answer with confidence and try not to get flustered. If the employer tries to unbalance you, remember it is an interview tactic to see how well you handle stress and how fast you are on your feet. Never hesitate and never retract previous statements. Employers harshly judge people who cannot make up their minds or take a stand. Many equate uncertainty with instability or incompetence, traits employers find undesirable. Never lose your cool. Think before talking, and answer with confidence and authority.

People hire people they like. Show some interest in the interviewer and the company. Always be courteous. Learn the interviewer's name and use it. However do not use his or her first name unless instructed to do so.

Finally, do not cover up your nervousness by talking too much. Listen when the interviewer speaks. Do not interrupt. If you have a question, wait until the interviewer has finished talking.

Illegal Questions

Sometimes an interviewer will ask an illegal question such as, "Are you married?" Sometimes an interviewer is just making small talk to relax you. Occasionally, it is an illegal screening device.

Usually not making an issue of the matter is the best strategy. If you become angry, you will probably not get the job. If you feel you have been discriminated against, you can bring a lawsuit. However be forewarned, you will have a difficult time proving you did not get the job due to discrimination. Worse yet, if you get a reputation as being difficult you may find it impossible to get any job.

The best thing to do is to dispel the employer's worry, and answer, "Yes, I am married, but my family totally supports my career decisions and I never let my family life affect my job performance." If the question is one that truly upsets your sensibilities, you may simply ask the interviewer to explain how the information he or she requests is relevant to the job at hand. This will usually stop the interviewer from proceeding with similar questions.

AFTER THE INTERVIEW

Questions *You* Should Ask

At the end of the interview, you may be asked if you have any questions. Even if you are not asked directly, you should interject, "Do you mind if I ask a few questions?" Asking questions shows that you are genuinely interested in the position.

However, you will be judged by your questions. Therefore, do not ask about salary and promotions. The interviewer may get a negative message that you are interested mainly in the paycheck. Additionally, do not ask what the organization or department does. A question like this shows you did'nt care enough about the interview to learn beforehand.

Ask questions about *the job*. This will display your interest and will supply you with the information you will need to decide if the job is right for you.

Questions you may want to ask include:

↷ To whom will I report?

↷ How do you see your company developing over the next few years?

↷ Is this a new position or will I be replacing someone?

↷ What happened to the last person who held this position?

↷ How many people have held this position in the last five years?

↷ What would be your highest priority for me to accomplish if you hired me?

Leaving the Interview

The interview is not over until you have left the premises. Offer a firm handshake and leave on a positive note. Express your thankfulness to the interviewer, complimenting him or her, and mentioning that you are eagerly looking forward to hearing from him or her.

One more note: always be courteous to the secretaries and assistants. For example, both upon entering and leaving the interview extend courtesies to the secretaries. Often they will be asked for their opinion about a candidate, so show respect to everyone you meet.

Taking Notes—A Retrospective

Immediately upon leaving the interview, take out your workbook. Be sure you have the correct spelling of the interviewer's name. Make notes on how you feel the interview went. What do you think could have made it better? Note any questions that stumped you. Be prepared for both the second stage and your next interview.

CHAPTER 18 THE JOB INTERVIEW ● 165

Checking Your References

If the interviewer is interested in hiring you, he or she will check your references. Understand that your former boss will be asked questions such as the following:

➙ How long has the applicant worked for you?

➙ How was the quality of the applicant's work?

➙ How did the applicant get along with you? With fellow workers?

➙ How much supervision did the applicant require?

➙ Who else could I talk to about the applicant?

The Follow-Up

Immediately upon returning home from the interview, write a follow-up, thank-you letter. Look at the sample letters in Chapter 13.

The letter should include two components. The first paragraph should be a courteous thank you for the interview. The second paragraph should reiterate why you want the job and what you can do for the company. It can be a recap of something you stressed during the interview or a new angle you thought of after the interview. Close with a statement that expresses your enthusiasm.

Wait one week and follow up with a phone call. If you do not get the job, ask the employer candidly for some constructive criticism on your interview technique. Note it in your workbook. This can greatly assist in preparing for future interviews.

THE MOCK INTERVIEW

The best way to prepare for an interview is to conduct a mock interview. Have a friend play the role of the employer and ask you the following questions. Record your answers on audio or videotape. Do not study the suggested answers yet. Listen to the playback. Compare your answers with the suggested answers. How do your answers compare?

Grade yourself on such qualities as your ability to communicate, confidence, enthusiasm, energy level, and intelligence. On videotape you can also judge such things as whether you maintained eye contact, smiled during the interview, fidgeted, sat straight, were attentive to the interviewer, and came across as someone you would like and could trust.

FREQUENTLY ASKED INTERVIEW QUESTIONS

Describe a typical working day.

Do your research and know the skills that are required in the job for which you are interviewing. Construct your answer to emphasize those skills in describing your typical day. Paint a picture of yourself as a hard worker, a problem solver, and an enthusiastic person.

For example, if the job you are seeking requires accuracy in report writing, you might say: "I spend much of my day writing reports. I put in significant effort checking and double checking. I always want to be 100 percent positive that everything is accurate."

Why are you interested in working for us?

Stress the company's excellent reputation and the exciting direction it is taking. Here your research will come in handy. Cite impressive things you have heard or read about the company. You may emphasize how well you feel you will fit in with the company's image and expectations.

If the company is small and does not have an outstanding reputation, you will want to stress that you enjoy working for small companies where you can distinguish yourself. If you have done your research and understand how your skills can benefit this particular company's needs, suggest that in your answer too.

What is your major weakness?

Do not be foolish enough to say you do not have any. Everyone has weaknesses. The idea is to mention one weak spot you are working at straightening. "I used to take on too many projects at once. Recently I attended a seminar on time management and I've found myself being more productive than ever."

Or you may mention a weakness that can be viewed in a positive light. For example: "I'm a workaholic and a perfectionist. I don't rest until the job is done as best as I can possibly do." These types of weaknesses are actually advantages for the employer.

Tell me about yourself. What are your greatest strengths?

This is not a biographical question. Your answer should stress your skills and abilities. "I'm a hard worker," "I'm a person with a good eye for detail," "I enjoy a job that lets me use my talents," are good answers. You may want to emphasize some of the major projects you worked on and the successes you have had. You may choose to talk about how you put yourself through school by working. Regardless, everything you tell about yourself should pertain to the job at hand and project a professional image.

What do you think of your previous boss?

Never be critical. Never complain. Doing so will tag you as trouble. Be positive and say something such as "I respect my former boss and learned a lot from him. I am seeking other employment because the opportunities for growth at my former company are limited."

Where do you see yourself five years from now?

The employer wants to be certain your plans do not include leaving the company after being trained. Emphasize your desire to be part of a winning team and to remain with them. You may say, "I plan to be here, advancing my career, and making satisfying accomplishments."

Tell me about your education. What subjects did you excel in?

Stress those subjects and areas of study that directly pertain to the job at hand. Mention stories and projects that demonstrate you have drive, possess motivation, and take initiative to do jobs properly.

Give a definition of a . . . (job title you are interviewing for).

The definition should be task oriented, defined by the responsibilities and accomplishments expected. For example, a data processor is someone responsible for accurately entering data so that meaningful reports and money-saving decisions will be produced.

What do you like to do in your spare time?

Mention activities that supplement and enhance your career goals. Examples are attending workshops, reading trade magazines, and attending conventions. You may want to include activities that show you care about your health and well-being, such as exercise and fitness classes. Steer away from anything political or controversial.

Why were you fired from your last job?

Do not lie. Many people will tell the interviewer that they were released due to cut-backs. Remember, this information can be easily verified in a short phone call to your last employer. Do not talk negatively about your former employer or coworkers, as this sort of negativism will ruin your chance of getting the job.

Explain what happened and take responsibility for your mistakes. However, be sure to tell the interviewer what you learned and gained from the experience and why you are now a better employee.

You may also qualify your termination by stating something like, "They needed someone who was more skilled in the area of _____" or "My interests and strengths lie more in the area of _____" (mention a strength that is crucial in the job for which you are interviewing).

What do you know about our company?

If you have done your research, this is where you can shine. If you have not, minimally try to impress upon the interviewer that you made an earnest albeit unsuccessful, attempt to gather information.

If the company has been in business for many years, you can honestly say, "Because I plan to stick with one company for a long time, I seek out stable companies with a strong reputation, such as yours."

What can you do for us that other candidates cannot?

Stress the benefits you can offer to the employer, your qualifications, and your ability to save the employer money. Be sure to stress some of your marketable personality traits, such as being a team player, a quick learner, and having strong communication skills (see Chapter 1). Stress your loyalty, dedication, and desire to remain with one company for the duration of your career.

How would you describe your personality?

Again, stress the positive. Describe the self-management skills you possess that would be most desired for your job, such as an ability to be a team player, an eye for accuracy, an ability to maximize time, and your honesty and integrity (see Chapter 1 for a list).

What interests you most about this job?

If you are aware of specific problems that you will be required to solve, mention those and explain that the *challenge* of solving these problems and the *opportunity to contribute* to the company excites you. If this job offers *more responsibility,* you could mention that, too.

Do you work better alone or in a group?

Again, researching and understanding the nature of the job at hand is crucial. If the job you are interviewing for requires working in a team, then obviously the answer to this question is working in a group. The employer is looking for you to assure him or her that you are a team player.

Why have you changed jobs so frequently?

Two approaches exist for answering this question. You can stress that your job changes were a result of your desire to gain diverse experience and develop a multitude of skills. Holding different positions was a growing experience that has given you a broader awareness of the workforce than most candidates. Be careful not to mention money as the prime motivating factor in changing jobs.

Another approach is to explain that you needed to try different careers before you could settle down with the one best suited for you. Tell the employer you are now confident you have made the choice for your future and are ready to settle down with one company and one job.

How much money do you want to make?

Never give a specific figure. You may price yourself out of the job or, worse yet, you may undersell yourself. Be vague. Answer with a general range, such as "Between $25,000 and $30,000 dollars."

Alternatively, you could ask outright, "What does the job pay?" After hearing the employer's answer, you can add that the pay is within the range or ballpark figure you had in mind.

ADDITIONAL QUESTIONS FOR RECENT GRADUATES

- ↱ Why did you attend _____ (your college or career school)?
- ↱ Why did you major in _____?
- ↱ What was your Grade Point Average (GPA)?
- ↱ Why were your grades so low? Did you do your best?
- ↱ What would you change about your education if you could?
- ↱ How did you finance your education?
- ↱ Tell me about some of your accomplishments.
- ↱ What extracurricular activities did you participate in?

Use the following worksheets to prepare for your interviews.

CHAPTER 18 / **W O R K S H E E T**

The Job Interview

Preparing for the Interview

COMPANY NAME: _____

POSITION: _____

DATE OF INTERVIEW: _____

TIME OF INTERVIEW: _____

PHONE NUMBER: _____

EMPLOYER'S (INTERVIEWER'S) NAME: _____

ADDRESS: _____

_____

TRAVELING INSTRUCTIONS: _____

_____

_____

TRAVEL TIME: _____

COMPANY DESCRIPTION (Background–Products–Services): _____

_____

_____

_____

_____

COMPETITORS: _____

SKILLS REQUIRED FOR THE JOB (compare want ad): _____

_____

_____

_____

CONTRIBUTIONS I CAN MAKE: _____

_____

_____

_____

SALARY RANGE: _____

(continued)

The Job Interview

Interview Checklist

- ☐ Resume—3 copies
- ☐ References
- ☐ Letters of recommendation
- ☐ Professional briefcase or portfolio (to hold everything)

- ☐ Business cards
- ☐ Samples of work
- ☐ Writing pad and pen

After the Interview

QUESTIONS THAT WERE DIFFICULT: _____

_____

_____

_____

_____

_____

_____

_____

_____

_____

INTROSPECTION (How I did or how I could improve my interview):

_____

_____

_____

_____

_____

_____

_____

_____

_____

_____

Follow-Up Checklist

- ☐ Thank-you letter
- ☐ Second phone call

- ☐ Phone call
- ☐ Second interview

Final Outcome

_____

_____

_____

The Job Interview

Preparing for the Interview

COMPANY NAME: _____

POSITION: _____

DATE OF INTERVIEW: _____

TIME OF INTERVIEW: _____

PHONE NUMBER: _____

EMPLOYER'S (INTERVIEWER'S) NAME: _____

ADDRESS: _____

_____

TRAVELING INSTRUCTIONS: _____

_____

_____

TRAVEL TIME: _____

COMPANY DESCRIPTION (Background—Products—Services): _____

_____

_____

_____

_____

COMPETITORS: _____

SKILLS REQUIRED FOR THE JOB (compare want ad): _____

_____

_____

_____

CONTRIBUTIONS I CAN MAKE: _____

_____

_____

_____

SALARY RANGE: _____

(continued)

The Job Interview

Interview Checklist

- ☐ Resume—3 copies
- ☐ References
- ☐ Letters of recommendation
- ☐ Professional briefcase or portfolio (to hold everything)

- ☐ Business cards
- ☐ Samples of work
- ☐ Writing pad and pen

After the Interview

QUESTIONS THAT WERE DIFFICULT: _____

_____

_____

_____

_____

_____

_____

_____

_____

_____

INTROSPECTION (How I did or how I could improve my interview):

_____

_____

_____

_____

_____

_____

_____

_____

_____

Follow-Up Checklist

- ☐ Thank-you letter
- ☐ Second phone call

- ☐ Phone call
- ☐ Second interview

Final Outcome

_____

_____

_____

CHAPTER 18 / WORKSHEET

The Job Interview

Preparing for the Interview

COMPANY NAME: _____

POSITION: _____

DATE OF INTERVIEW: _____

TIME OF INTERVIEW: _____

PHONE NUMBER: _____

EMPLOYER'S (INTERVIEWER'S) NAME: _____

ADDRESS: _____

_____

TRAVELING INSTRUCTIONS: _____

_____

_____

TRAVEL TIME: _____

COMPANY DESCRIPTION (Background–Products–Services): _____

_____

_____

_____

_____

COMPETITORS: _____

SKILLS REQUIRED FOR THE JOB (compare want ad): _____

_____

_____

_____

CONTRIBUTIONS I CAN MAKE: _____

_____

_____

_____

SALARY RANGE: _____

(continued)

The Job Interview

Interview Checklist

☐ Resume—3 copies
☐ References
☐ Letters of recommendation
☐ Professional briefcase or portfolio (to hold everything)

☐ Business cards
☐ Samples of work
☐ Writing pad and pen

After the Interview

QUESTIONS THAT WERE DIFFICULT: _____

_____

_____

_____

_____

_____

_____

_____

_____

_____

INTROSPECTION (How I did or how I could improve my interview):

_____

_____

_____

_____

_____

_____

_____

_____

_____

_____

Follow-Up Checklist

☐ Thank-you letter
☐ Second phone call

☐ Phone call
☐ Second interview

Final Outcome

_____

_____

_____

YOUR PERSONAL JOB JOURNAL

TWO PURPOSES OF THE JOURNAL

This personal job journal is designed to meet two goals.

➢ to help you generate a list of potential employers

➢ to track your progress with your target market

GENERATING A TARGET MARKET LIST

To create a constructive list of employers (those looking to hire someone with your credentials), you will have to endure some preliminary steps. Secondary contacts will lead you to primary contacts, which will after some effort result in a master list: your target market.

SECONDARY CONTACTS/RESEARCH

Record the names of friends and acquaintances who can assist you. Ask them to supply you with the names of people in your field that they personally know. If they do not know anyone, minimally get the names of other people they know who can help you.

Use your library's resources to get the names of employees at all local businesses in your field. Try to determine which person at each firm is in charge of hiring. Record these leads as primary contacts.

PRIMARY CONTACTS

Any business or organization that employs people in your field is a primary contact. Call all of these businesses. Learn if they are hiring and what plans they have. Try to reach the person in charge of hiring—even if no job is presently available. Introduce yourself to that person. If you were referred to him or her by one of your secondary contacts, mention that person's name.

Even if no job is available, ask if you can send a copy of your resume for future reference. Better yet, set up an informational interview. Move any primary contact that expresses an interest in you to your master list—target market.

If a primary contact shows no interest, ask if they know someone else who is looking to hire. If they do, write that person's name on your list of primary contacts. Contact that person next, mentioning the name of the person who just referred you to him or her. Names carry weight, so use them whenever possible.

WEB CONTACTS

You will want to keep a paper trail of everyone you have contacted on the Web. This includes e-mail addresses and the URL address of any company or job board that you frequent. The Web is an incredible maze, and it's all too easy to forget which sites were helpful. *Document everything.*

Pay particular attention to those Web sites where you posted your resume. Record the date you posted your resume and how long it will stay on that particular job board. Tag or number (code) each version of your resume, and include each one in your job search portfolio. Make a note of which version you posted on which sites. You can enter the version code on your contact sheet also, and thus easily track which version of your resume you sent to whom.

Similarly, track which online ads you answered. Print out the ads for your job search portfolio and code them. On your job journal contact sheet, enter the code under the heading "Job Description and Number," making it easy to track which job postings you answered.

MASTER LIST—TARGET MARKET

From your list of primary contacts (those you have phoned) select those who indicated an interest in you and record them on your master list. Concentrate on these contacts. They are the employers who are most likely to hire you.

Strategize. Write what you can do for each company in a tailored cover letter. Be sure each of the contacts on your master list gets a copy of your resume with a personalized cover letter. Better yet, set up a meeting with the person in charge of hiring. Do not be a nuisance, but follow up often enough that he or she will remember you. Anytime a primary contact expresses interest in you, he or she becomes a member of your target market, and you should record him or her on your master list.

WANT ADS ANSWERED

Although you should not place too much faith in want ads, answering a legitimate ad never hurts. Keep track of the ads you have answered and the date. Follow up if possible, and record all results. Add any employer that shows an interest in you to your master list, even if he or she does not hire you. Follow up later.

WEEKLY/MONTHLY PLANNER

Be organized. Set aside time daily to make calls and send out resumes and cover letters. Record all your activities: meetings, phone calls, and resumes sent. Additionally, record all your tasks, such as follow-up letters and phone calls that you must make at later dates, as well as any scheduled interviews. Most importantly, check your calendar every morning.

KEEP FINDING CONTACTS AND KEEP MAKING CALLS. BE PERSISTENT AND YOU WILL GET A JOB SOONER THAN YOU THINK!

SECONDARY CONTACTS

Think of at least 15 people—friends, relatives, business associates, organization members, anyone—who can supply you with leads (names of potential employers). Write their names below and get their phone numbers. Call them. On your list of Primary Contacts record the names of potential employers they give you.

	Name	Phone Number	✓ Done
1.			
2.			
3.			
4.			
5.			
6.			
7.			
8.			
9.			
10.			
11.			
12.			
13.			
14.			
15.			
16.			
17.			
18.			
19.			
20.			
21.			
22.			
23.			
24.			
25.			

RESEARCH SOURCES

Write down the titles of resource materials (Web sites, directories, Yellow Pages–headings, trade journals, and periodicals) that you will check for leads. Ask your librarian for assistance. Check these sources for the names of companies and/or people hiring. Again, enter all *potential* employers on your list of Primary Contacts.

	Sources	✓ Done
1.		
2.		
3.		
4.		
5.		
6.		
7.		
8.		
9.		
10.		
11.		
12.		
13.		
14.		
15.		
16.		
17.		
18.		
19.		
20.		
21.		
22.		
23.		
24.		
25.		

WANT ADS ANSWERED

Name of the Firm	Address or Blind Box #	Name and Date of Publication of Ad	Date Answered	Results

PRIMARY CONTACTS

Name of the Firm	Phone Number	Contact's Name and Title	Referred to By (Person/Source)	Results

PRIMARY CONTACTS

Name of the Firm	Phone Number	Contact's Name and Title	Referred to By (Person/Source)	Results

PRIMARY CONTACTS

Name of the Firm	Phone Number	Contact's Name and Title	Referred to By (Person/Source)	Results

CONTACTS MADE ON THE WEB

Name	Address	Phone	E-mail Address	Web Site

RESUMES POSTED ON THE WEB

Board	URL	Post Date	Expiration Date	Resume Version

JOB POSTS ANSWERED ON THE WEB

Board	Date	Job Description and Number	Destination URL

MASTER LIST—TARGET MARKET

Call Number	Contact's Name & Title	Phone Number	Firm's Name and Address	Dates of Action					Results
				Resume	Meeting	Letter	Follow Up	Follow Up	
1.									
2.									
3.									
4.									
5.									
6.									
7.									
8.									
9.									
10.									
11.									
12.									
13.									

MASTER LIST–TARGET MARKET

Call Number	Contact's Name & Title	Phone Number	Firm's Name and Address	Dates of Action					Results
				Resume	Meeting	Letter	Follow Up	Follow Up	
1.									
2.									
3.									
4.									
5.									
6.									
7.									
8.									
9.									
10.									
11.									
12.									
13.									

WEEKLY PLANNER

MONTH: _____ WEEK # _____		
To Do:	**Phone Calls / Meetings / etc.**	**✓ Done**
Mon:	8:00	
	9:00	
	10:00	
	11:00	
	12:00	
	1:00	
	2:00	
	3:00	
	4:00	
	5:00	
Tues:	8:00	
	9:00	
	10:00	
	11:00	
	12:00	
	1:00	
	2:00	
	3:00	
	4:00	
	5:00	
Wed:	8:00	
	9:00	
	10:00	
	11:00	
	12:00	
	1:00	
	2:00	
	3:00	
	4:00	
	5:00	
Thur:	8:00	
	9:00	
	10:00	
	11:00	
	12:00	
	1:00	
	2:00	
	3:00	
	4:00	
	5:00	
Fri:	8:00	
	9:00	
	10:00	
	11:00	
	12:00	
	1:00	
	2:00	
	3:00	
	4:00	
	5:00	

WEEKLY PLANNER

MONTH: _____ **WEEK #** _____

To Do:			Phone Calls / Meetings / etc.	✓ Done
Mon:		8:00		
		9:00		
		10:00		
		11:00		
		12:00		
		1:00		
		2:00		
		3:00		
		4:00		
		5:00		
Tues:		8:00		
		9:00		
		10:00		
		11:00		
		12:00		
		1:00		
		2:00		
		3:00		
		4:00		
		5:00		
Wed:		8:00		
		9:00		
		10:00		
		11:00		
		12:00		
		1:00		
		2:00		
		3:00		
		4:00		
		5:00		
Thur:		8:00		
		9:00		
		10:00		
		11:00		
		12:00		
		1:00		
		2:00		
		3:00		
		4:00		
		5:00		
Fri:		8:00		
		9:00		
		10:00		
		11:00		
		12:00		
		1:00		
		2:00		
		3:00		
		4:00		
		5:00		

MONTHLY PLANNER

Sunday	Monday	Tuesday	Wednesday	Thursday	Friday	Saturday

P = Phone Call   R = Resume   L = Letter   I = Interview

MONTHLY PLANNER

Sunday	Monday	Tuesday	Wednesday	Thursday	Friday	Saturday

P = Phone Call   R = Resume   L = Letter   I = Interview

SECONDARY CONTACTS

Think of at least 15 people—friends, relatives, business associates, organization members, anyone—who can supply you with leads (names of potential employers). Write their names below and get their phone numbers. Call them. Record on your list of Primary Contacts the names of potential employers they give you.

	Name	Phone Number	✓ Done
1.			
2.			
3.			
4.			
5.			
6.			
7.			
8.			
9.			
10.			
11.			
12.			
13.			
14.			
15.			
16.			
17.			
18.			
19.			
20.			
21.			
22.			
23.			
24.			
25.			

RESEARCH SOURCES

Write down the titles of resource materials (Web sites, directories, Yellow Pages–headings, trade journals, and periodicals) that you will check for leads. Ask your librarian for assistance. Check these sources for the names of companies and/or people hiring. Again, enter all *potential* employers on your list of Primary Contacts.

	Sources	✓ Done
1.		
2.		
3.		
4.		
5.		
6.		
7.		
8.		
9.		
10.		
11.		
12.		
13.		
14.		
15.		
16.		
17.		
18.		
19.		
20.		
21.		
22.		
23.		
24.		
25.		

WANT ADS ANSWERED

Name of the Firm	Address or Blind Box #	Name and Date of Publication of Ad	Date Answered	Results

PRIMARY CONTACTS

Name of the Firm	Phone Number	Contact's Name and Title	Referred to By (Person/Source)	Results

PRIMARY CONTACTS

Name of the Firm	Phone Number	Contact's Name and Title	Referred to By (Person/Source)	Results

PRIMARY CONTACTS

Name of the Firm	Phone Number	Contact's Name and Title	Referred to By (Person/Source)	Results

CONTACTS MADE ON THE WEB

Name	Address	Phone	E-mail Address	Web Site

RESUMES POSTED ON THE WEB

Board	URL	Post Date	Expiration Date	Resume Version

JOB POSTS ANSWERED ON THE WEB

Board	Date	Job Description and Number	Destination URL

MASTER LIST—TARGET MARKET

Call Number	Contact's Name & Title	Phone Number	Firm's Name and Address	Dates of Action						Results
				Resume	Meeting	Letter	Follow Up	Follow Up	Follow Up	
1.										
2.										
3.										
4.										
5.										
6.										
7.										
8.										
9.										
10.										
11.										
12.										
13.										

MASTER LIST–TARGET MARKET

Call Number	Contact's Name & Title	Phone Number	Firm's Name and Address	Dates of Action					Results
				Resume	Meeting	Letter	Follow Up	Follow Up	
1.									
2.									
3.									
4.									
5.									
6.									
7.									
8.									
9.									
10.									
11.									
12.									
13.									

WEEKLY PLANNER

MONTH: _____ **WEEK #** _____

To Do:			Phone Calls / Meetings / etc.	✓ Done
Mon:		8:00		
		9:00		
		10:00		
		11:00		
		12:00		
		1:00		
		2:00		
		3:00		
		4:00		
		5:00		
Tues:		8:00		
		9:00		
		10:00		
		11:00		
		12:00		
		1:00		
		2:00		
		3:00		
		4:00		
		5:00		
Wed:		8:00		
		9:00		
		10:00		
		11:00		
		12:00		
		1:00		
		2:00		
		3:00		
		4:00		
		5:00		
Thur:		8:00		
		9:00		
		10:00		
		11:00		
		12:00		
		1:00		
		2:00		
		3:00		
		4:00		
		5:00		
Fri:		8:00		
		9:00		
		10:00		
		11:00		
		12:00		
		1:00		
		2:00		
		3:00		
		4:00		
		5:00		

WEEKLY PLANNER

MONTH: _____ **WEEK #** _____

To Do:			Phone Calls / Meetings / etc.	✓ Done
Mon:		8:00		
		9:00		
		10:00		
		11:00		
		12:00		
		1:00		
		2:00		
		3:00		
		4:00		
		5:00		
Tues:		8:00		
		9:00		
		10:00		
		11:00		
		12:00		
		1:00		
		2:00		
		3:00		
		4:00		
		5:00		
Wed:		8:00		
		9:00		
		10:00		
		11:00		
		12:00		
		1:00		
		2:00		
		3:00		
		4:00		
		5:00		
Thur:		8:00		
		9:00		
		10:00		
		11:00		
		12:00		
		1:00		
		2:00		
		3:00		
		4:00		
		5:00		
Fri:		8:00		
		9:00		
		10:00		
		11:00		
		12:00		
		1:00		
		2:00		
		3:00		
		4:00		
		5:00		

MONTHLY PLANNER

	Sunday	Monday	Tuesday	Wednesday	Thursday	Friday	Saturday

P = Phone Call   R = Resume   L = Letter   I = Interview

MONTHLY PLANNER

Sunday	Monday	Tuesday	Wednesday	Thursday	Friday	Saturday

P = Phone Call   R = Resume   L = Letter   I = Interview

INDEX